TO THE ENDS
OF THE EARTH

LEGACY

TO THE ENDS
OF THE EARTH
LEGACY

MARK C. MCCANN

Our
Sunday
Visitor

www.osv.com
Our Sunday Visitor Publishing Division
Our Sunday Visitor, Inc.
Huntington, Indiana 46750

Our Sunday Visitor Publishing Division
Our Sunday Visitor, Inc.
200 Noll Plaza
Huntington, IN 46750
1-800-348-2440

ISBN: 978-1-68192-388-8 (Inventory No. T2269)
eISBN: 978-1-68192-389-5
LCCN: 2018959300

Cover design: Tyler Ottinger
Cover art: Shutterstock
Interior design: Lindsey Riesen

PRINTED IN THE UNITED STATES OF AMERICA

To my father-in-law, Gerald Davino, who taught me that a Catholic man is both a strong leader and a solid friend, a tireless and tender provider for his family, and a serious and sober defender of the Faith. You are a true follower of Christ — a believer with an open heart, a humble worldview, and a willingness to grow as a man of God. Thank you for being a shining example of Christian manhood and for accepting me into your family. Thank you most of all for nurturing the daughter who became my beautiful bride and shared God's salvation story with me.

TABLE OF CONTENTS

PREFACE

As men we are all about making our mark in the world. As Catholic men, we need to consider exactly what that means with regard to our faith in Christ and our membership in his Church. We are on a journey along a narrow road, moving ever forward toward the Kingdom of God. How we live will stand as a testimony for others who will come after us.

The kind of legacy we leave behind is not simply a matter of saying the "right words" or doing the "right things." It involves our whole lives — our thoughts and desires, our sweat and our labors, our relationships and our goals. If we are focused on Christ and him alone, the kind of testimony that our lives will speak will reflect his glory to all the world.

During the next ten weeks, we will be looking at what it means to be a man of legacy. Throughout this study, we will focus on our calling to grow as individuals and as brothers in Christ, always keeping in mind the goal of adding to the great and glorious story of salvation and to our call to lead others to heaven's gates.

This book is both a personal daily devotional and a tool for group study with other men. Each day, you are encouraged to read through the day's devotion, pray and meditate on the message from God's word, and reflect on the questions provided, always remembering the theme for the week and seeking to apply it to your life. It is suggested that you take fifteen to thirty minutes in the morning to complete each devotion, and then let your prayerful experience with the Lord guide you throughout your day.

On Saturday, you are encouraged to look back on your week of study, reflecting on the progress you've made, thanking God for the work he has done in your life, throwing any mistakes into the ocean of God's mercy, and committing to personal goals in areas where you'd like to see improvement in the coming week.

For those who want to take things a step further, you are encouraged to keep a journal where you write your reflections, track your progress in Christian living, and dialogue with the God who is leading you on this journey of manhood. You can then use your journal to help you share your insights and discoveries with other men.

The key to growing with this study involves two things: taking time to read and learn each day, and then living out the message through practical acts of love. This means taking the reflection questions and turning them into action steps that you can do as you love your family, serve your church and community, and lift up your brothers in the Faith.

Once a week, you are encouraged to come together with other Catholic men to share your thoughts on the devotions, the insights you have gained in prayer, and the ways you have put these principles into practice in everyday life. The leader of your study group will facilitate a discussion, focusing on those passages, reflections, and actions that have meant the most to the men in the group. After a general sharing of thoughts about the daily devotions, the leader can focus on the Saturday "Go Deeper" questions. As each man shares ideas, the leader will encourage the other men to build on the ideas raised and add their own unique voice to the discussion.

As you make this journey, determine to spend more time in prayer, study, and worship to grow in your faith. Look for opportunities to interact with your brothers, as you build one another up, carry one another's burdens, and hold one another accountable before God. Love your families and your communities with the same uncompromising love that Christ has poured out onto you. Look for ways to make this world a better place by being a man who represents Christ and his Church well. Look forward to all the blessings that are to come in God's good time!

INTRODUCTION

THE LOVE WE LEAVE BEHIND

The world as we know it is passing away.

There is, however, an eternal inheritance awaiting us in heaven. As we travel on the road of salvation, we follow in the footsteps of the saints who have previously walked the narrow way. Our inheritance in the Kingdom of God has been secured for us by the cross of Christ, a holy birthright that we are called to pass on to the generations of believers who will come after us. The legacy of our Catholic faith is a heavenly one, grounded in Christ and lived out in our daily lives as we move from faith to faith, with our eyes ever fixed on the prize that awaits us in the kingdom yet to come.

We hope to one day look back upon our lives and see the blessings that have come through the steps we have taken and the choices we have made. We must ask ourselves whether we have brought joy into sorrow, peace into struggle, and wisdom into uncertainty. Have our families, our friends, and our Church been made richer because they bear the imprint of our lives? Will our contributions to the Catholic Church, large and small, lead others closer to the One who came to set them free? Will the words we have spoken and the actions we have taken result in a more blessed family reunion around the banquet table at the heavenly wedding feast? These are questions each of us must be willing to ask as we live our lives.

We have power to share the blessings of our faith with this world, to live lives of honesty and integrity, casting off falsehood in favor of gospel truth. Committing to the cause of Christ puts us in the thick of the battle, where our faith is tested time and time again. Jesus never promised an easy life to those who believed. In fact, he told us we would face trouble, division, persecution, and even death for the sake of the kingdom. Yet God also assures us that he will never leave us or forsake us (cf. Heb 13:5), and that he has wonderful, prosperous plans for our lives (cf. Jer 29:11). We who believe can rest assured that when the world around us is shaking to its very foundations, God remains the unshakable, all-powerful Lord of the glad city of heaven.

This is what leaving a legacy is all about. In Christ, we are born into a new life from above, gifted and empowered to carry out our purpose for the Kingdom of God, and joined to a community of faith so that we may support one another and build up the body of believers. We are called to draw the lost into the family of faith, to grow as individuals, and to become all that we have been called to become. Everything we do should reveal to the world that we are but pilgrims on this earth, walking in faith straight into the heavenly places. When we have left this world for the world to come, our greatest joy should be that when people looked at us, they saw Jesus and him alone.

During this ten-week study, we will consider the challenge of the Gospel to place our mark upon the world and to shape the Church that has so beautifully shaped each of us. Every aspect of our lives as Christians is meant to carry out the Great Commission of making disciples, baptizing them and teaching them as Jesus has taught us, and resting on the final promise that Jesus will be with us to the end of the age (cf. Mt 28:16–20). Let all you read and consider and pray over in the days to come lead you to a greater awareness of how you are helping to ready the Bride of Christ for the day when the Bridegroom comes again to call her to the Wedding Feast.

WEEK 1

THE BEST-LAID PLANS . . .

Do not boast about tomorrow,
*   for you do not know what a day may bring forth.*
He who tends a fig tree will eat its fruit,
*   and he who guards his master will be honored.*
Know well the condition of your flocks,
*   and give attention to your herds;*
for riches do not last for ever;
*   and does a crown endure to all generations?*
Proverbs 27:1, 18, 23–24

Men tend to like order. When we make plans, we like to stick to them. We are also providers who want to make sure our families have what they need. Yet in this broken world of ours, situations change, human beings can be fickle, and unpredictable events pop up all the time. Just when we think everything is fine, a sudden illness comes along, a friend falls away, our employment changes, or some other disaster strikes. These realities teach us that to rely on our best-laid plans places us on shaky ground.

Though we are but dust and ashes, God enables us to live our lives and make plans for the future — plans that impact not just us, but those who will come after us as well. Yet, ultimately, God is in charge of everything, including the course of our lives and the legacy we leave behind. Still, we are called to be attentive to our responsibilities as Catholic men. This week, we will reflect on how we are to strike the balance between making plans and trusting God. We will consider the following points:

1. God cares about our efforts and rewards them.

While God is all-powerful and does not need our help (cf. Acts 17:25), he still calls us to take care of ourselves and those he has placed in our care. We have his promise that, if we are faithful to him, we will reap the harvest of our efforts and experience God's provision.

2. God is the power that binds all things together.

We may feel we have control of our lives, but God alone is before all things and holds everything together (cf. Col 1:17). We have the power to make plans and direct our actions only because God has given it to us. Instead of relying on our own strength to prepare for our future, and for the generations that will follow us, we must rely on God alone.

3. God directs all things for good.

Often as we make our own plans, we forget that God's plan for us is bolder, bigger, and much better than we could ever imagine. God has planned a future full of hope and not harm for his people (cf. Jer 29:11). We can trust that he directs all things for good (cf. Rom 8:28), knowing that our fear and doubt will give way to faith in the unfolding of his perfect will.

4. God's purposes for our lives prevail.

We make many plans, but in the end it is God's will that will stand (cf. Prv 19:21). We live, we work, and we plan for our future; yet in everything, God's eternal and perfect will still comes to pass. He loves us that much.

5. We have no cause for worry.

God's plan was never designed to cause us anxiety or fear. As we work to find our place and leave our mark in this life, we can allow the daily worries to give way to childlike trust, knowing God greatly desires to provide all that we need to complete the journey he has set for us.

This Week's Call to Action

This week, be mindful of the sovereign God who calls us to journey toward tomorrow while relying on him to see us through. Though we have no guarantee of our next breath, we exist, we prosper, and we gain heaven all because of the love of God given to us in Christ. Thank God for his guidance and provision. Let your plans be centered on his promises and commands. Serve him by seeking his will and living it out in all you say and do. Take time for prayer, study, fellowship, and worship throughout the week.

As you interact with others, remember that nothing is a surprise to God. Nothing is beyond the scope of his will and his power to work all things out according to his divinely laid plans. Let this precious truth calm your fears and guide your steps as you work out your legacy and look toward a future where lives are changed, joy flows freely, and hope reveals itself in the plans that God has laid out for you.

SUNDAY

This week we will reflect on God's sovereignty, and we will practice surrendering our plans before him in trusting submission. God calls each of us to lay our life before his throne, believing in his perfect plan. God cares about our efforts and rewards them, for he is the source of all good things. His plans prevail, and his plans are good. Yielding to those plans is the starting point to leaving a lasting legacy that will reflect the beauty, the grace, and the glory of the One who enables you to act to shape the Church and the world for good.

As you celebrate the Eucharist this Sunday, bring your plans into the church building and lay them down before the altar. As you listen to the readings, be mindful of the story of salvation and how, from the very beginning, God has been working all things out to the good. Thank him that you have been included in his plan of salvation and made a part of his Church. Consider how God's plan has unfolded in your life and how your life is a reflection of the great love of Jesus, who died on the cross for your sins. As you receive the Eucharist, let the wonderful truth that God loves you that much sink deeply into your soul. Reflect on where you think your life is going and what plans you believe God still has for you. Thank him for his love and promise him that you will continue to live your life in trust, submission, and joy.

Questions for reflection

Do you find it difficult to yield to God's plans? What are the parts of your life where this is hardest for you?

What practical steps can you take this week to start living in total surrender to God's perfect, loving will?

Praying with Scripture

"Commit your work to the LORD, / and your plans will be established" (Prv 16:3).

MONDAY
GOD CARES ABOUT OUR EFFORTS AND REWARDS THEM

Then the King will say to those at his right hand, "Come, O blessed of my Father, inherit the kingdom prepared for you from the foundation of the world; for I was hungry and you gave me food, I was thirsty and you gave me drink, I was a stranger and you welcomed me, I was naked and you clothed me, I was sick and you visited me, I was in prison and you came to me." Then the righteous will answer him, "Lord, when did we see you hungry and feed you, or thirsty and give you drink? And when did we see you a stranger and welcome you, or naked and clothe you? And when did we see you sick or in prison and visit you?" And the King will answer them, "Truly, I say to you, as you did it to one of the least of these my brethren, you did it to me."

Matthew 25:34–40

God wants us to lay up our treasures in heaven (cf. Mt 6:20). We must be careful, then, about how we build upon the foundation he has laid in our lives, working out our salvation with fear and trembling (cf. Phil 2:12). God allows our efforts to produce real fruit in our lives and in the lives of those who come after us. In the end, his cleansing fire will reveal what that fruit has been (cf. 1 Cor 3:13), and we will receive God's reward for our efforts.

What we do matters, not only because God allows our actions to have an impact on the world, but because as Christians we are called to do all for his glory. The deeds we do on earth determine the reward we will receive from God. Let us remember that our service — especially to the least in God's kingdom — also leaves a legacy for future generations.

Questions for reflection
Are you laying up your treasure in heaven, or are you sometimes tempted to plan only for the needs of this life?

How are you connecting your works of mercy with God's overall plan for your life?

Where have you seen your labors produce real fruit in the life of someone else?

Praying with Scripture

"Whatever your task, work heartily, as serving the Lord and not men, knowing that from the Lord you will receive the inheritance as your reward; you are serving the Lord Christ" (Col 3:23–24).

TUESDAY
GOD IS THE POWER THAT BINDS ALL THINGS TOGETHER

Come now, you who say, "Today or tomorrow we will go into such and such a town and spend a year there and trade and get gain"; whereas you do not know about tomorrow. What is your life? For you are a mist that appears for a little time and then vanishes. Instead you ought to say, "If the Lord wills, we shall live and we shall do this or that." As it is, you boast in your arrogance. All such boasting is evil.

James 4:13–16

God is God and we are not. This means our plans must give way to the perfection of his will. We often believe that we have total control over our lives and that everything is up to us. While we can and should make important decisions about our lives, we must accept that we are dependent on the Lord for our next breath. God is truly the author and perfecter of our faith (cf. Heb 12:2). Our lives and our plans are completely in his hands.

By recognizing that God is the source of all we do, we align our actions to his will. This brings us great freedom from worry and enables us to move forward, trusting in his sovereign care for our lives. It gives us confidence, strength, and purpose in all we do, allowing us to respond to his commands with joy and hope for the future. We know that our lasting legacy is in heaven, not here on earth.

Questions for reflection

Is it hard for you to relinquish control of your life? What are some of the areas where this is hardest for you, and why?

Has there been a time in your life when yielding to God's will brought you prosperity and peace?

What are some upcoming decisions in your life that you need to give over to God's care?

Praying with Scripture

"He is before all things, and in him all things hold together" (Col 1:17).

WEDNESDAY
GOD DIRECTS ALL THINGS FOR GOOD

For I know the plans I have for you, says the LORD, plans for welfare and not for evil, to give you a future and a hope. Then you will call upon me and come and pray to me, and I will hear you. You will seek me and find me; when you seek me with all your heart.

Jeremiah 29:11–13

Just as God spoke peace into the life of the prophet Jeremiah, so too does he assure us of his perfect care for every detail of our existence. We can remain hopeful about the future, whatever it might hold. Ultimately, God has the greatest good in store for us: the glory of his eternal presence

It can be easy to forget, as we get caught up in our own plans, that God has a plan, and his plan includes us. We can trust absolutely in the goodness of God's design. Those of us who are fathers have seen the trust that our children have in us. They are willing to follow our direction and learn from us because they know we love them and have their best interests at heart. In the same way, we must respond to God the Father like little children, each day taking new steps toward the goals our heavenly Father has set for us. Let us take those steps with joy, knowing our Father is directing all things to the good for those of us who love him (cf. Rom 8:28).

Questions for reflection

What parts of your life are you still trying to handle on your own?

How has your relationship with God shaped your decisions about the future?

This week, how can you help a brother who struggles to trust in God's good plans?

Praying with Scripture

"A man's mind plans his way, / but the LORD directs his steps" (Prv 16:9).

THURSDAY
GOD'S PURPOSES FOR OUR LIVES PREVAIL

I am God, and there is none like me,
declaring the end from the beginning
    and from ancient times things not yet done,
saying, "My counsel shall stand,
    and I will accomplish all my purpose,"
calling a bird of prey from the east,
    the man of my counsel from a far country.
I have spoken, and I will bring it to pass;
    I have planned, and I will do it.

Isaiah 46:9–11

Isaiah spoke these words to assure God's people that the Lord would use the powerful pagan leader Cyrus (whose symbol was an eagle) to restore them to their homeland. The Jews had been taken into captivity because of their sins, yet God's purposes for their lives would stand. He would bring about the victory. His promise to the ancient Israelites also pointed forward to the coming of Christ, the ultimate source of our salvation. We are part of a wonderful story, spoken into existence from eternity, carried out according to the perfect will of Almighty God.

Just as God has brought us salvation in Jesus, so he guides every aspect of our lives. We sin and stumble on the way, but we can never upset God's perfect plan. In spite of everything, his plan prevails and will prevail. As we take our many daily decisions and lay them at the throne of God's grace, we can be certain that he will bring them to fruition according to his wonderful design. What an awesome blessing it is to be able to participate in such a wonderful legacy of love and faithfulness!

Questions for reflection
Have you seen God's purposes for your life unfold even through unusual circumstances? What were those circumstances?

How has learning to trust God changed your relationship with him?

What good work is God doing in your life today that will have a lasting impact on the world?

Praying with Scripture
"Many are the plans in the mind of a man, / but it is the purpose of the LORD that will be established" (Prv 19:21).

FRIDAY
WE HAVE NO CAUSE FOR WORRY

And he said to his disciples, "Therefore I tell you, do not be anxious about your life, what you shall eat, nor about your body, what you shall put on. For life is more than food, and the body more than clothing. Consider the ravens: they neither sow nor reap, they have neither storehouse nor barn, and yet God feeds them. Of how much more value are you than the birds! And which of you by being anxious can add a cubit to his span of life? If then you are not able to do as small a thing as that, why are you anxious about the rest? Consider the lilies, how they grow; they neither toil nor spin; yet I tell you, even Solomon in all his glory was not clothed like one of these. But if God so clothes the grass which is alive in the field today and tomorrow is thrown into the oven, how much more will he clothe you, O men of little faith! And do not seek what you are to eat and what you are to drink, nor be of anxious mind. For all the nations of the world seek these things; and your Father knows that you need them. Instead, seek his kingdom, and these things shall be yours as well."

Luke 12:22–31

We need never worry about tomorrow. All the concerns of life, important as they are, are under God's care and control. God wants to give us what we need, and he always gives it to us joyfully. Even in the midst of our deepest trials, he is there, loving us and providing the strength we need to see the journey through to the end. For our part, he asks only that we trust him for all our needs. We can bring him every pain and sorrow and celebrate every joy with him.

Often we shape our plans around our security and our happiness, forgetting that we have no real control over our future. God, however, has our very lives in his hands. In Christ, we can live free from the cares and concerns about what is to come, and by yielding to God's care, accomplish great things for the Kingdom of God. There is no need God cannot meet and no situation he cannot work according to his will for those who seek first his kingdom and his righteousness.

Questions for reflection
When has God taken your anxiety and worry and brought you comfort and peace?

What are some earthly treasures you might be holding a little too close to your heart?

What can you do to allow God's will to unfold more freely in your life and the lives of those you meet?

Praying with Scripture
"We know that in everything God works for good with those who love him, who are called according to his purpose" (Rom 8:28).

SATURDAY

Go Deeper
Do I believe that God wants to give me good things? Are there parts of my life where I struggle to trust in his goodness?

_____

_____

_____

_____

_____

Have I surrendered my plans to God's perfect plans, or am I clinging to certain designs and hopes of my own?

_____

_____

_____

_____

_____

_____

Do I seek God's glory in everything that I do, or are some of my plans motivated by selfishness?

_____

_____

_____

_____

_____

_____

What parts of my life do I need to surrender to the care of my heavenly Father?

_____

_____

———————————————————————————

———————————————————————————

———————————————————————————

———————————————————————————

Has God brought good out of my struggles in the past? What were those struggles, and what was their outcome? How can I use those experiences to grow in trust?

———————————————————————————

———————————————————————————

———————————————————————————

———————————————————————————

———————————————————————————

Have I helped others trust more completely in God, or have my words and actions contributed to anxiety and lack of trust? What can I do to assist those around me who struggle to trust in God's plans?

———————————————————————————

———————————————————————————

———————————————————————————

———————————————————————————

WEEK 2

WHEN THINGS FALL APART

God is our refuge and strength,
a very present help in trouble.
Therefore we will not fear though the earth should change,
though the mountains shake in the heart of the sea;
though its waters roar and foam,
though the mountains tremble with its tumult.

Psalm 46:1–3

These are troubling times. We face war, terrorism, deep political and ideological divisions, and a host of struggles that tear at the fabric of our society and challenge our Catholic faith. It can be overwhelming at times. As men, we wish we could face these fights head on and find real solutions and lasting peace; but no matter what we do, things seem to be getting worse.

It is difficult to see how struggles are a part of the legacy we will leave behind.

No matter what happens, God is in control of our lives. He is the rock upon which our faith stands. Keeping this truth in focus allows us to let go and accept our need for God. This week, we will reflect on five core truths about God's presence and action in our lives.

1. The shaking of the earth does not shake God.

Psalm 46 contrasts the rock-steady strength of the Lord with the raging "temper tantrum" of the earth. Even when it seems that all is falling apart around us, we can always look to the One who never is shaken.

2. God's presence remains rock-steady.

Not only is God powerful, he is powerfully present in our world and in each of our lives. He never leaves us, for he is the rock that can never be moved. No matter what we face today, God remains our refuge in the storm.

3. God brings stillness to our troubled times.

Even in our greatest moments of struggle, God's promises can bring an overwhelming sense of peace to our hearts. He is our refuge, and in his arms we find rest from our weariness and recovery from our sorrow.

4. With a word, God can bring the fury of our fight to an end.

The daily battles we fight, some serious and some less so, can cause us to become caught up in a spirit of conflict and forget that we are traveling to a hopeful future where all wars and all conflicts will cease. If we listen carefully, we can hear the Lord whispering a word that will bring our restless fight to a peaceful resolution.

5. We live in the City of God.

Even in the chaos and violence of the world, we can look to the City of God, where we hope to live for all eternity. We begin our communion in the heavenly city even now, as members of the Church founded by Jesus Christ.

This Week's Call to Action

When we are struggling with loss, illness, division, sin, or pride, and when the world and its institutions are crumbling before our very eyes, we can rest in the perfect truth that God forever remains our refuge and our strength. This week, strive to find your steady place in the midst of life's storms. Find ways to invite the power and presence of God into the chaos of life. Spend time with your Father, talking about your fears and struggles.

Knowing that God brings good out of our trusting surrender — not just for us, but for everyone in our lives — helps us to move forward along the stream of salvation to the place where all the noise and clamor of life will give way to the voice of our Savior calling us home. This week, let surrender guide your steps every day. Allow God's eternal will to draw you closer to Christ and his Church. Reflect on the future happiness to which you are called by your faith in Jesus, and let God show you the role he wants you to play in bringing souls to this same happiness.

SUNDAY

This week, we will consider God's faithfulness in our lives, no matter the circumstances we face. God remains a rock of refuge who causes the battles of our lives to give way to peace and surrender. God has a heavenly city in store for all who follow him. As believers, we live within that city right now. God loves his people, and that love shines before us to light our way and manifests itself perfectly in the life of the Church, leading us on to our heavenly inheritance.

This Sunday at Mass, listen for the conflicts in the story of salvation, the struggles the People of God faced. As you celebrate the Eucharist, remember that Jesus went to the cross to bring us salvation and to complete our story. Pray about this story, thank God for the good he has done for humanity from the beginning, the good he has done in your life, and the good that is to come when Jesus returns to judge the living and the dead. Let these awesome truths guide you as you go forth to love others and leave a legacy of faith for all the world to see.

Questions for reflection
When in your life have you seen most clearly that God was your rock?

What chaos and upheavals in the world (and your small part of it) cause you the most distress, and how can you draw nearer to God for support and hope?

Praying with Scripture
"The salvation of the righteous is from the LORD; / he is their refuge in the time of trouble" (Ps 37:39).

MONDAY
THE SHAKING OF THE EARTH DOES NOT SHAKE GOD

In you, O LORD, I seek refuge;
    let me never be put to shame;
    in your righteousness deliver me!
Incline your ear to me,
    rescue me speedily!
Be a rock of refuge for me,
    a strong fortress to save me!
Yes, you are my rock and my fortress;
    for your name's sake lead me and guide me,
take me out of the net which is hidden for me,
    for you are my refuge.
Into your hand I commit my spirit;
    you have redeemed me, O LORD, faithful God.

Psalm 31:1–5

Trials and earthshaking tribulations do not shake the Lord, who is our rock of refuge. Though this world is full of sin and falsehood, acts of evil and human misery, God remains our deliverer and our stronghold. He cannot be moved by the forces that work to undermine the Church and our freedom in Christ. Yet his heart is moved by compassion and mercy to rescue his people from the persecution of enemies and the worship of worthless idols. God knows our distress and lifts us up, guiding us into the kingdom of his Son.

We know all too well that our lives can be shaken by the smallest difficulties. When we feel oppressed and distressed, we can be confident that we have refuge in the One who always remains the same. Our confidence is an integral part of what it means to be men who leave a lasting legacy. How we rest on the rock-solid promises of Christ leaves a powerful example for those around us, particularly our children and our family of faith. It stands as a testimony of the strength and faithfulness of our good God.

Questions for reflection

What are some of the trials you face (or see) that trouble you the most?

When have you experienced God's strength and guidance in the midst of trials?

How can you share the strength of Jesus Christ with another who is struggling today?

Praying with Scripture

"For who is God, but the LORD? And who is a rock, except our God?" (2 Sm 22:32).

TUESDAY
GOD'S PRESENCE REMAINS ROCK-STEADY

And the LORD went before them by day in a pillar of cloud to lead them along the way, and by night in a pillar of fire to give them light, that they might travel by day and by night; the pillar of cloud by day and the pillar of fire by night did not depart from before the people.

Exodus 13:21–22

God remains ever-present in the midst of chaos and disaster. Our all-powerful Savior goes before the Church, guiding her in strength toward the promised land. He is our beacon of hope, our powerful protector, by day and night. He will never fail nor forsake his people.

No matter what we face in our individual lives or as members of the Body of Christ, we know that God is with us. He will see us through this journey of salvation until the day we share our lives with him forever in heaven. His strength, his Spirit, his light, and his love become ours as we carry on the legacy of other faithful followers who have shown forth the presence of God through their lives. Let us remember that God will keep us from falling and lift us to heights of joy. He will remain our rock of refuge forever!

Questions for reflection

Where do you experience God's guiding presence in your life and in the life of the Church?

How does the knowledge that God will neither leave nor forsake you give you strength and hope?

How can you respond to someone who feels God has abandoned them or the Church?

Praying with Scripture

"For he has said, 'I will never fail you nor forsake you'" (Heb 13:5).

WEDNESDAY
GOD BRINGS STILLNESS TO OUR TROUBLED TIMES

Open the gates,
  that the righteous nation which keeps faith
  may enter in.
You keep him in perfect peace,
  whose mind is stayed on you,
  because he trusts in you.
Trust in the LORD for ever,
  for the LORD GOD
  is an everlasting rock.

Isaiah 26:2–4

All of us at some point in our lives will face personal struggles, whether they be physical, emotional, financial, or relational. It's not something we can avoid. In fact, Jesus warned us that we would face such trials; but he also promised that we could rest cheerfully because he has overcome the world (cf. Jn 16:33). Such promises help to sustain us when we face the tough times and fear we will falter under the pressure. God opens the door to his powerful presence and brings us to a place of peace.

God may not remove our troubles right away (or at all), but we can believe that he loves us and is working out our salvation through each and every circumstance. As we weather the storms of life and strive to seek the face of God when life throws its worst at us, we become caught up in the peace of Christ. We can then focus our minds on the place where those who trust in God come to dwell. We become part of the ongoing story of recovery, righteousness, and rest, a story that shines upon the world and lights the way for all those who will come after us.

Questions for reflection

When have you experienced the perfect peace of God in the midst of a difficult struggle?

Why is it important to keep our faith strong and focus our minds on the peace of God when we are facing trials and tribulations?

How can you bring the precious presence of Christ into the life of a brother who is struggling today?

Praying with Scripture

"And he awoke and rebuked the wind, and said to the sea, 'Peace! Be still!' And the wind ceased, and there was a great calm" (Mk 4:39).

THURSDAY
WITH A WORD, GOD CAN BRING THE FURY OF OUR FIGHT TO AN END

Peace I leave with you; my peace I give to you; not as the world gives do I give to you. Let not your hearts be troubled, neither let them be afraid.

John 14:27

May the LORD give strength to his people!
May the LORD bless his people with peace!

Psalm 29:11

When we struggle with conflict in our lives, it can lead to a spirit of anger, resentment, fear, or despair. These things can overwhelm us and shut down the good we are called to do.

We need to remember that Jesus longs to speak peace into our hearts. When God speaks a word to us, it has the power to come alive. When he tells us to "Be not afraid," we can truly lay aside all fear. When he says, "Peace be with you," peace enters our hearts. He wants to lift us up from our struggles and conflicts and bring us to a heavenly place where we see these conflicts for what they are. From heaven's heights our earthly struggles seem small indeed.

We who have experienced the perfect peace of Christ know that we have the strength to overcome the obstacles of life and turn the journeys through our struggles into a living sign of the power of God to bring peace to our souls. Like the mighty saints of old, our faith stories become a testament of wisdom that we can pass on to those who will go through similar struggles in their lives.

Questions for reflection
When has God caused you to stop struggling or to give up your conflicts in favor of his lasting peace?

When you face trials, do you seek the Word that will bring the fury of your fight to an end?

What word can you speak to someone dealing with conflict in his life?

Praying with Scripture
"When the cares of my heart are many, / your consolations cheer my soul" (Ps 94:19).

FRIDAY
We Live in the City of God

Great is the LORD and greatly to be praised

in the city of our God!
His holy mountain, beautiful in elevation,
    is the joy of all the earth,
Mount Zion, in the far north,
    the city of the great King.
Within her citadels God
    has shown himself a sure defense.
As we have heard, so have we seen
    in the city of the LORD of hosts,
in the city of our God,
    which God establishes for ever.

Psalm 48:1–3, 8

Through the storms of life, believers can take comfort that in the future we will enter the eternal City of God. No matter how much we struggle, God promises us that the violence and chaos of life will give way to eternal life in a city so beautiful, so secure, that we will never worry or experience sin or sadness again.

Even now on earth, Catholics experience the City of God within the Church. She is our beautiful refuge from the struggles of life, a fortress of righteousness and joy, the source of our nourishment in the sacraments. We can be assured that she will stand from now until the time when Our Lord comes again to judge the living and the dead. In her we see the victory that is ours in Christ, and we can share this Good News with generations to come.

Questions for reflection

How does this vision of our heavenly Jerusalem help you to live in freedom today?

What is the most beautiful aspect of the Catholic Church that gives you comfort and peace?

What are you passing on to future generations of believers to give them the hope of heaven?

Praying with Scripture

"For he looked forward to the city which has foundations, whose builder and maker is God" (Heb 11:10).

SATURDAY

Go Deeper

Do I trust in God's power when things in my life seem to be falling apart, or do I try to weather the storms on my own?

_____

_____

_____

_____

Have I surrendered my trials to God this week? If not, what do I need to lay at his feet?

_____

_____

_____

Do I realize that heaven is my inheritance, and live my life for that goal, or have I allowed storms and troubles to distract me?

_____

_____

_____

_____

How has God shown me his love and power this week? Have I thanked him for his providence?

_____

_____

_____

Do I live with an eternal perspective, knowing that God can cause the chaos of my life to give way to the perfect peace of his kingdom?

_____

_____

_____

_____

How can I accompany a brother who is undergoing trials or storms right now?

_____

_____

_____

WEEK 3

Our Legacy Is One of Hope

*Then I saw a new heaven and a new earth; for the first heaven
and the first earth had passed away, and the sea was no more.
And I saw the holy city, new Jerusalem, coming down out of
heaven from God, prepared as a bride adorned for her husband; and I heard a great voice from the throne saying, "Behold, the dwelling of God is with men. He will dwell with them,
and they shall be his people, and God himself will be with them;
he will wipe away every tear from their eyes, and death shall be
no more, neither shall there be mourning nor crying nor pain
any more, for the former things have passed away."*

Revelation 21:1–4

The world seems to be getting worse instead of better. People
are divided politically, culturally, and spiritually. There are wars
and rumors of wars, poor people suffering all over the globe,
and selfishness and sin at an all-time high. It might seem like
God has forgotten us, but Jesus talked about this extensively (cf.
Matthew 24). It is all part of living in a broken world.

Still, we can take courage. Our legacy as Christians is a legacy of hope. The cross brought salvation and began the Church.
We are on a journey through the storms of history with the
heavenly throne room in sight. The Church has gone through
her infancy and adolescence and is coming into maturity as her

people continue to fight the good fight of faith.

What can we as Catholic men take away from God's Word concerning our hopeful future? This week we will consider the following points:

1. The new is coming and the old will pass away.

We sometimes forget that the way the world is now is not how it will always be. Jesus promises that there will be a new heaven and a new earth where all the evils of the past will vanish away. Because this new and eternal life is our legacy, we can look forward with expectation and hope.

2. Like a bride, the Church is being readied for her wedding.

In the early Church, a bride was given a ceremonial bath before her wedding. Now, Jesus is purifying the Church, his Bride, for the great wedding feast that is to come. We are marching down the aisle as we prepare to meet our heavenly groom.

3. God will dwell with his people in the world to come.

Some have forgotten that Jesus came to live with us and will one day bring us to live with him forever. We need to reclaim this great mystery, take hold of it with joy, and never let go.

4. Our tears and our struggles will be nothing compared to the hope that is to come.

Creation is groaning as in labor, awaiting its redemption in the new birth to come (cf. Rom 8:18–25). In Jesus, we have been given the first fruits of heaven through the cross. The best is yet to come!

5. We will pass through the rising waters and the raging fire and find heaven.

No matter how heavy and difficult they may be, the trials we face now shall not sweep us away or consume us (cf. Is 43:2). The power that raised Christ from the dead lives in us and is carrying the People of God to our final home, our New Jerusalem.

This Week's Call to Action

One of the greatest obstacles we face in bringing people to Christ is giving an answer for the struggles of this world. As Catholics, we need to proclaim the powerful truth that the best is yet to come, so that others can discover the same hope that is ours.

We proclaim this truth first of all in the way we live. We know we can hold on through the storms of life because we can trust the One who holds the lightning in his hand (cf. Jb 36:32) and calms every storm (cf. Lk 8:22–25).

This week, focus your prayers, your speech, and your actions on the hope we have in Christ. Consider what it means to belong to the Church, the Bride of Christ, who is readying herself for the Bridegroom. Let that shape how you respond to the sin, sadness, and falsehood you experience in the world. Strive to show love, to trust that the end of the story is in God's hands, and to know that all our concerns can be laid at the feet of our God, who is all-powerful and all-loving.

SUNDAY

This week, pray, reflect, and act on your legacy as a Christian man: a legacy of hope. Everything you possess here on earth will one day give way to new heavens and a new earth. Each of us as baptized Christians has a role in preparing the Church, the Bride of Christ, to meet her Bridegroom. When that day comes, God will dwell with his people forever, and nothing you can experience in this life can compare to the riches of the world to come.

As you celebrate the Mass this Sunday, meditate on how the Eucharist is God's perfect expression of his love for you in Christ, and how it points to the kingdom to come. Think about how the parts of the Mass here on earth mirror the great Wedding Feast that is celebrated in eternity. Consider how this great truth and your own journey through your trials will help to shape how you prepare the Bride of Christ for her wedding as you serve within the Church.

Questions for reflection
How can you see your struggles in light of the promises of what is to come?

How can you help a brother see his trials and difficulties in the light of hope this week?

Praying with Scripture
"Hear, O daughter, consider, and incline your ear; / forget your people and your father's house; / and the king will desire your beauty. / Since he is your lord, bow to him" (Ps 45:10–11).

MONDAY
THE NEW IS COMING AND THE OLD WILL PASS AWAY

The Lord is not slow about his promise as some count slowness, but is forbearing toward you, not wishing that any should perish, but that all should reach repentance. But the day of the Lord will come like a thief, and then the heavens will pass away with a loud noise, and the elements will be dissolved with fire, and the earth and the works that are upon it will be burned up. Since all these things are thus to be dissolved, what sort of persons ought you to be in lives of holiness and godliness, waiting for and hastening the coming of the day of God, because of which the heavens will be kindled and dissolved, and the elements will melt with fire! But according to his promise we wait for new heavens and a new earth in which righteousness dwells. Therefore, beloved, since you wait for these, be zealous to be found by him without spot or blemish, and at peace.
                                                        2 Peter 3:9–14

Because of our fallen nature, we can sometimes become too attached to this earth and too focused on the here and now. We forget that God promises that the old order of things will pass away, and we will witness new heavens and a new earth. Right now, because of Adam's sin, the world is subject to decay. The proof of this is all around us, yet we still cling to the things of this world as if they will always be with us.

This is not how Christian men are supposed to live. The passing away of the earth should not be our main concern. Rather, we need to focus on how we are to live. Living in hope means striving to lead holy lives devoted to God as we wait patiently for and "hasten" the day of Christ's coming. We must strive for heaven, eagerly awaiting what God has in store for us.

Questions for reflection
What parts of your life tend to keep you earthbound rather than bound for heaven?

Is God's promise of new heavens and earth real to you? What can you do to remind yourself of this reason for hope in your daily life?

How can you help a brother surrender an earthly attachment and focus his eyes on heaven?

Praying with Scripture
"And the world passes away, and the lust of it; but he who does the will of God abides for ever" (1 Jn 2:17).

TUESDAY
LIKE A BRIDE, THE CHURCH IS BEING READIED FOR HER WEDDING

Then I heard what seemed to be the voice of a great multitude,

like the sound of many waters and like the sound of mighty
thunderpeals, crying

> "Hallelujah! For the Lord our God the Almighty reigns.
> Let us rejoice and exult and give him the glory,
> for the marriage of the Lamb has come,
> and his Bride has made herself ready;
> it was granted her to be clothed with fine linen, bright and
> pure" —

for the fine linen is the righteous deeds of the saints. And the
angel said to me, "Write this: Blessed are those who are invited
to the marriage supper of the Lamb." And he said to me, "These
are true words of God."

Revelation 19:6–9

On the day of his wedding, a groom waits at the altar as his bride walks down the aisle to join him in the Sacrament of Matrimony. She wears a spotless white gown, a symbol of her purity as she gives herself forever to the one who will be her husband. Like a bride preparing for her wedding with a ceremonial bath and a white wedding gown, the Bride of Christ is being purified by her trials and putting on her garment of righteousness so she will be ready for the Bridegroom, Jesus Christ.

As members of the Church, we are called to prepare the Bride of Christ for her wedding. This is part of the legacy we leave behind. How we live as Catholic men helps to shape the Church for what is to come, including her trials. We need to ask ourselves how we are contributing to the Church's growth and maturity. Are we devoted to Christ alone? Are we striving to live spotless lives, free from the stain of sin? If we take our baptism seriously, we will see our role within the Church as something vital to her future. Our legacy is inseparable from the legacy of the Church.

Questions for reflection

How can you work to devote yourself more fully to the Body of Christ?

What does the Church need to do right now to ready herself for the Bridegroom?

How ready do you feel today to be called to the wedding feast of the Lamb?

Praying with Scripture
"For your Maker is your husband, / the LORD of hosts is his name; / and the Holy One of Israel is your Redeemer, / the God of the whole earth he is called" (Is 54:5).

WEDNESDAY
GOD WILL DWELL WITH HIS PEOPLE IN THE WORLD TO COME

For behold, I create new heavens
*   and a new earth;*
and the former things shall not be remembered
*   or come into mind.*
But be glad and rejoice forever
*   in that which I create;*
for behold, I create Jerusalem a rejoicing,
*   and her people a joy.*
I will rejoice in Jerusalem,
*   and be glad in my people;*
no more shall be heard in it the sound of weeping
*   and the cry of distress.*
*   Isaiah 65:17–19*

The beautiful poetic language of this passage from Isaiah gives us a glimpse into the joy, peace, and glory that we will experience when Jesus comes again. All of the sorrows and struggles of this life will one day be no more. The One who came to dwell with us as man will come again to judge the living and the dead. We who believe will dwell with him in a joyful eternity.

The Kingdom of God is among us now; yet we see sin, division, sorrow, and evil of all kinds. Still, the spread of the Gospel continues as the Church journeys ever forward to the day when the Bride will be forever joined to the Bridegroom at the wedding feast of the Lamb. The perfection and goodness to come cannot be fully grasped, but we do know it will be wonderful, joyful, and everlasting. God will dwell with his people forever. This should strengthen us and empower us to live as kingdom participants, always seeking the will of God, living in the grace and love of the One who gave himself up to death on the cross and who continues to give himself to us in the Eucharist.

Questions for reflection

How does knowing that the earth as we know it will pass away help you to live for the glory of heaven?

How often do you offer praise to the One who will create new heavens and a new earth?

How can you offer this blessed hope to those who are steeped in sorrow and suffering today?

Praying with Scripture

"My dwelling place shall be with them; and I will be their God, and they shall be my people" (Ez 37:27).

THURSDAY
OUR TEARS AND OUR STRUGGLES WILL BE NOTHING COMPARED TO THE HOPE THAT IS TO COME

I consider that the sufferings of this present time are not worth comparing with the glory that is to be revealed to us. For the creation waits with eager longing for the revealing of the sons of God; for the creation was subjected to futility, not of its own will but by the will of him who subjected it in hope; because the creation itself will be set free from its bondage to decay and obtain the glorious liberty of the children of God. We know that the whole creation has been groaning with labor pains together until now; and not only the creation, but we ourselves, who have the first fruits of the Spirit, groan inwardly as we wait for adoption as sons, the redemption of our bodies. For in this hope we were saved. Now hope that is seen is not hope. For who hopes for what he sees? But if we hope for what we do not see, we wait for it with patience.

Romans 8:18–25

The best is yet to come. We have heard this phrase, but for many it does not seem true. Some are struggling in their marriages, failing at their careers, and in despair over their sense of worth. The world seems to be going from bad to worse, and so many are caught up in suffering and chaos, as creation and humanity groan, shedding tears and calling out for redemption and restoration.

Yet we as Catholics can remain firmly rooted in the hope of that phrase. The best is yet to come because our Savior came down from heaven and redeemed his people through the cross. He died in our place, formed his Church, and is walking with her on her journey toward the new birth that is to come. We have been given the first fruits of the resurrection of Our Lord. We groan during this life on earth because we recognize that there is another world to come. While we cannot see it with our eyes, we experience it through the eyes of faith (cf. Heb 11:1). Because of this, we wait with patient endurance for our final redemption that is to come, and work out our salvation for our good and the glory of God.

Questions for reflection

What are some of the deepest sorrows you see in your life and the world around you today? How do these sorrows affect your hope?

How has Christ helped you to endure as you wait for the kingdom to come?

How does your hope in heaven shape how you live as a member of the Church?

Praying with Scripture

"He will swallow up death for ever, and the Lord GOD will wipe away tears from all faces, and the reproach of his people he will take away from all the earth, for the LORD has spoken" (Is 25:8).

FRIDAY
WE WILL PASS THROUGH THE RISING WATERS AND THE RAGING FIRE AND FIND HEAVEN

But now thus says the LORD,
* he who created you, O Jacob,*
* he who formed you, O Israel:*
Fear not, for I have redeemed you;
* I have called you by name, you are mine.*
When you pass through the waters I will be with you;
* and through the rivers, they shall not overwhelm you;*
when you walk through fire you shall not be burned,
* and the flame shall not consume you.*
For I am the LORD your God,
* the Holy One of Israel, your Savior.*

Isaiah 43:1–3

When we go through trials, sometimes it may feel as though God has abandoned us and that the suffering we are enduring will consume us. Yet as we have considered time and time again in this study, God strengthens us in our trials and allows them to shape us for the kingdom. Jesus warns us that in this life we will have troubles. But we can take courage because he has overcome the world (cf. Jn 16:33).

God is with us through our trials. The One who has re-deemed us and called us by name walks with us through the rising waters and the raging fires of adversity. He will not allow our struggles to consume us. Rather, he refines us in the fires of trials so that our faith may be made genuine and our lives will be a source of praise, glory, and honor when Jesus is re-vealed. We must remember that we were created to reflect per-fectly the glory of God. We are called to rise above and press on through the sorrows of this life so that we can become saints who radiate the glory of our heavenly Father for all eternity.

Questions for reflection
How has the testing of your faith made you a more genuine Catholic man?

What is one thing you have learned from witnessing God's grace in the midst of trials?

How does living for the glory of God change your whole per-spective on your worth?

Praying with Scripture
"Blessed is the man who endures trial, for when he has stood the test he will receive the crown of life which God has prom-ised to those who love him" (Jas 1:12).

SATURDAY

Go Deeper

Do I live for the world to come, or am I too deeply attached to the good things of this world?

_____

_____

_____

_____

Do I recognize that I am part of the Bride of Christ? Have I been doing my part to prepare her for the Bridegroom?

_____

_____

_____

_____

Have I allowed my trials to strengthen and refine me, or have I given way to complaining and bitterness because of them?

_____

_____

_____

_____

Do I long for heaven and the kingdom that is to come, or do I seek after earthly joys without considering my eternal destiny?

_____

_____

_____

Do I pray for the Church? How can I begin to pray for the Church more regularly? What is one thing I can commit to now for the days and weeks ahead?

_____

_____

_____

_____

WEEK 4

SORROW AND HOPE

Man that is born of a woman is of few days, and full of trouble.
He comes forth like a flower, and withers;
    he flees like a shadow, and continues not.
Since his days are determined,
    and the number of his months is with you,
    and you have appointed his bounds that he cannot pass.
Oh, that you would hide me in Sheol,
    that you would conceal me until your wrath be past,
    that you would appoint me a set time, and remember me!
You would call, and I would answer you;
    you would long for the work of your hands.
For then you would number my steps,
    you would not keep watch over my sin;
my transgression would be sealed up in a bag,
    and you would cover over my iniquity.

Job 14:1–2, 5, 13, 15–17

Throughout history, man has struggled to understand the purpose of suffering. Perhaps no work of literature encapsulates this struggle as well as the biblical book of Job. As Job ultimately found, although suffering remains a mystery deep within the heart of God, we who experience our suffering in the presence of his perfect love can connect to its power and discover the hope that is ours in Christ.

Catholic men are not immune from struggle and pain. Our faith does not shield us from suffering and the grief that goes along with it. Yet if we are grounded in Christ, linked through the cross to the One who gave his life for our sins, we can weather the storms of life and find the peace that passes all our understanding. We can turn our trials into triumphs as we are transformed by the love of our Savior and join our story with the story of the Church's journey to maturity.

How do we discover comfort in the midst of trouble and hope in the midst of grief? Scripture is filled with passages showing how the experience of sorrow is transformed into hope through the perfect love of God. This week, we will look at these ideas:

1. Though we walk through the valley of the shadow of death, God is there (cf. Ps 23:4).

Our Lord is the One who leads us through our darkest days into the light of hope. He conquers the enemies around us and leads us to pastures where we receive his abundant comfort once more. Refreshed and renewed by God's grace, we take our place in God's holy dwelling, the Church, as we bring our uniqueness to bear upon her.

2. God preserves our lives from the pit (cf. Ps 30:1-6).

We rejoice because in Christ we have been rescued from hell and brought to a place where our enemies can boast no more. He has heard our cries for deliverance. Our tears of sorrow in the darkness of suffering give way to joyful living in the light of his love. As we are established in strength and new life, we become men who pour out our lives for the Body of Christ in songs of praise and acts of love that will carry on into eternity.

3. As we are comforted, so we will comfort others (cf. 2 Cor 1:3-5).

God pours out all his comfort and grace upon us in our troubles, making us strong enough to take that same comfort to others. Our sufferings are a sharing in the sufferings of Christ; our comfort too abounds and reaches out into the world to leave our mark through the same Jesus who has loved us to the full.

4. Those who mourn are blessed (cf. Mt 5:4).

Those who experience the sorrow of loss can find peace at the cross where Jesus experienced separation from the Father and bore every sin and every grief. Death no longer has its way with us because Jesus has conquered the grave and given us a new inheritance in heaven. We live no longer for ourselves, but for the One who has set us free.

5. God heals the brokenhearted and binds our wounds (cf. Ps 147:3).

While our suffering can seem like it will never end, God promises to heal our hearts and bind our wounds. He will not abandon us, but walks with us every step of the way on our journey of salvation. As we are made whole, we become healers to others, offering the story of our suffering as a testimony of God's grace. Our life becomes a legacy of healing that leads others to seek the One who will bind up their wounds as well.

This Week's Call to Action

There is a link between sorrow and hope that finds meaning in the transforming power of Christ and the cross. As you travel the road of salvation this week, focus on the ways Jesus helps you to overcome your sorrow and find greater blessings in your journey through it. Spend time in close meditation with your Savior, letting him take the heavy burdens from you and walk with you as you take up the light and easy load he offers. Find ways to ease the sorrows and sufferings of others as you share the grace you have received from the Savior who suffered to bring you new life.

Understanding how sorrow and hope are linked through Christ enables us to live out our Catholic faith in a powerful way. Our transformation from the depths of sorrow to the mountaintop of hope is an incredible witness of God's love and the power of his Church. It serves to inspire others and comfort them as they walk through the valley of sorrow as well.

SUNDAY

Though our sorrows can often overwhelm us, God pours out his presence into the lives of those who mourn. His perfect, intimate, and eternal love comes into your grief and lifts you up from the pit of despair. Allow the One who gave up his life for you to comfort and heal you. Then look for ways you can bring the message of hope to those around you who are suffering in sorrow.

This Sunday, let the readings at Mass, particularly the Gospel, speak to you about the healing love of Jesus Christ. Consider how Our Lord came to bring hope, strength, and joy to those who were hopeless, helpless, and full of sorrow. As you come to the table and receive the Eucharist, consider the greatest act of love that unfolds before you as the mystery of our salvation is played out upon the altar. Spend some time praying and (if you feel moved to do so) journaling about the sorrows and struggles in your life and how God, through his Son's death and resurrection, has brought you hope. Think of ways God has spoken words of healing to you through Scripture and your Catholic brothers. Thank God for his comfort and all the ways you are sharing that message of hope with others who experience sorrow and grief.

Questions for reflection

How has your journey through suffering shaped your faith?

How has the Lord shown you his presence and care in the midst of sufferings and trials?

How can you share the same comfort you have received with others today?

Praying with Scripture

"He will wipe away every tear from their eyes, and death shall be no more, neither shall there be mourning nor crying nor pain any more, for the former things have passed away" (Rv 21:4).

MONDAY
THOUGH WE WALK THROUGH THE VALLEY OF THE SHADOW OF DEATH, GOD IS THERE

Peace I leave with you; my peace I give to you; not as the world gives do I give to you. Let not your hearts be troubled, neither let them be afraid. You heard me say to you, "I go away, and I will come to you." If you loved me, you would have rejoiced, because I go to the Father; for the Father is greater than I. And now I have told you before it takes place, so that when it does take place, you may believe. I will no longer talk much with you, for the ruler of this world is coming. He has no power over me; but I do as the Father has commanded me, so that the world may know that I love the Father. Rise, let us go from here.

John 14:27–31

One of the most beautiful and amazing truths about Jesus is that, even though he was going to face one of the cruelest forms of torture ever devised and a spiritual anguish no other man could endure, he did so with total joy. In fact, the Bible says that Jesus despised the shame of the cross and took upon himself all our sins *for the joy before him* — his ultimate triumph over sin and death (cf. Heb 12:2). In his darkest hour, his love for his disciples — and for all of us — was first and foremost in his mind. He sought to do the Father's will out of love for humanity. He conquered death, hell, and the Devil, and brought comfort, peace, and salvation for all who would believe.

Jesus endured the pain of death so that he could leave us a lasting legacy of hope — a hope that can never fade. As we follow our Savior through the valley of the shadow of death, we know that he has paved the way to the resurrection. Our lives can forever be part of the story of salvation, the story of self-sacrifice and obedience to the Father's will. As we share in that story, we help to empower others to join in the story as well.

Questions for reflection
When have you experienced God's powerful presence in your darkest trials?

How does knowing that Jesus walks with you help you to overcome your struggles and experience the joy of submitting to the Father's will?

What are some practical ways you can offer God's comfort to someone who is longing for that same peace today?

Praying with Scripture
"Even though I walk through the valley of the shadow of death, / I fear no evil; / for you are with me; / your rod and your staff, / they comfort me" (Ps 23:4).

TUESDAY
GOD PRESERVES OUR LIVES FROM THE PIT

I waited patiently for the LORD;
*   he inclined to me and heard my cry.*
He drew me up from the desolate pit,
*   out of the miry bog,*

and set my feet upon a rock,
  making my steps secure.
He put a new song in my mouth,
  a song of praise to our God.
Many will see and fear,
  and put their trust in the LORD.

Psalm 40:1–3

The simple truth of humanity is that we were lost and unable to save ourselves, stuck in a pit of sin and despair and beyond hope. But the Son of God left his throne in heaven and came to earth to draw us up from that pit and set our feet on the right path toward heaven. He heard our cries for deliverance and restored us and put a song of praise in our mouths. That is why he has no equal!

Now we stand beside our brothers and live as members of a body of believers, working out our salvation and leading others into the Kingdom of God. As Catholic men, we need to learn how to appreciate that powerful reality and allow it to shape the way we live for God. Our lives should shine forth as beacons of light to those who will come after us, and all we do should contribute to the Church to which we belong.

Questions for reflection
How does knowing that you deserved hell but were given heaven influence how you live?

How often do you offer praise and thanksgiving to the One who redeemed you from the pit?

What message of hope are you leaving for those who long to be raised to new life?

Praying with Scripture
"I will extol you, O LORD, for you have drawn me up, / and have not let my foes rejoice over me" (Ps 30:1).

WEDNESDAY
AS WE ARE COMFORTED, SO WE WILL COMFORT OTHERS

The LORD is my light and my salvation;
whom shall I fear?
The LORD is the stronghold of my life;
of whom shall I be afraid?
When evildoers assail me,
to devour my flesh,
my adversaries and foes,
they shall stumble and fall.
Though a host encamp against me,
my heart shall not fear;
though war arise against me,
yet I will be confident.

Psalm 27:1–3

What happens when God shines his light on his children? Fear fades, enemies flee, and our flesh is freed. God deeply desires to give us the comfort that transforms our lives and makes us whole.

The strength that is ours in Christ helps us to overcome our sufferings and, in turn, give that same comfort to others. We have been given an eternal inheritance, and now we shine as light and stand strong in the midst of our enemies. Every soul we comfort with the grace that has been given to us adds to the glory of the Church. We are confident, comforted pillars of strength to others, part of God's fortress of faith because the Son of God has brought his light to our lives.

Questions for reflection
How has God comforted you in the face of fear of enemies, obstacles, and failures?

How are you leaving a legacy of love by the way you bring the light of Christ to bear upon the world?

What opportunities do you have to provide comfort to others, just as you have received comfort from God?

Praying with Scripture
"For as we share abundantly in Christ's sufferings, so through Christ we share abundantly in comfort too" (2 Cor 1:5).

THURSDAY
THOSE WHO MOURN ARE BLESSED

When the righteous cry for help, the LORD hears,
and delivers them out of all their troubles.
The LORD is near to the brokenhearted,
and saves the crushed in spirit.
Many are the afflictions of the righteous;
but the LORD delivers him out of them all.

Psalm 34:17–19

But this I call to mind,
and therefore I have hope:
The steadfast love of the LORD never ceases,
his mercies never come to an end;
they are new every morning;
great is your faithfulness.

Lamentations 3:21–23

No one escapes grief. The death of a loved one breaks our hearts and crushes our spirits. We experience trouble, struggles, shame, and disappointment. Our place within the Kingdom of God does not shield us from the pain of living in a broken world; but when we cry out, our prayers are heard. Our

Father is never far from his children, and he desires to deliver us from all our woes.

As Catholic men, we are blessed to belong to a family that forever experiences the unending mercy of our heavenly Father. We who mourn experience the comforting touch of the over-flowing presence of God. As we discover the hope that is ours in Christ, we are able to share that message of hope with others. We become shining examples of Christ's compassion, carrying on his legacy of healing and comfort as we add our own unique voice to the Church. Strengthened by the mercy of God, we can speak life to those who mourn, helping to transform their lives so that they too may leave their own special mark on the Body.

Questions for reflection

How has God comforted you with his unending mercy during your own times of mourning?

Where has God turned mourning into a renewing love in your family of faith?

How can you bless those who grieve by helping them to experience the comfort of Christ?

Praying with Scripture

"Blessed are those who mourn, for they shall be comforted" (Mt 5:4).

FRIDAY
GOD HEALS THE BROKENHEARTED AND BINDS OUR WOUNDS

For I will restore health to you,
and your wounds I will heal,
says the LORD,

because they have called you an outcast:
  "It is Zion, for whom no one cares!"
Thus says the LORD:
Behold, I will restore the fortunes of the tents of Jacob,
  and have compassion on his dwellings;
the city shall be rebuilt upon its mound,
  and the palace shall stand where it used to be.
Out of them shall come songs of thanksgiving,
  and the voices of those who make merry.
I will multiply them, and they shall not be few;
  I will make them honored, and they shall not be small.

Jeremiah 30:17–19

When we face our brokenness, it can feel as though our wounds will never heal. We feel lost, destroyed, out of options, and beyond hope. We wonder if God can fix us or if he is even there. Our lives are in a heap of ruins, seemingly never to be rebuilt. What can we do when we experience our woundedness?

The answer lies in the One who suffered to the fullest for the worst sins of humanity. Only Jesus can bring us new life, restore our fortunes, and heal our wounds. The glory in this is that Jesus not only heals us, he builds a beautiful new dwelling from our ruined lives. We are enabled to multiply the blessings of God by sharing the healing of God with others. No longer outcasts, we are citizens of heaven who now share an eternal inheritance and live with a new purpose in the Kingdom of God.

Questions for reflection
What wounds have you brought to the Lord for healing, and what was the result?

What kind of a dwelling has God created from the ruins of your life? How has that dwelling impacted the lives of others?

How can you celebrate God's restoration by helping to restore the lives of others?

Praying with Scripture

"The LORD builds up Jerusalem; / he gathers the outcasts of Israel. / He heals the brokenhearted, / and binds up their wounds" (Ps 147:2–3).

SATURDAY

Go Deeper

How has God shown me his great love in the midst of my suffering? Have I allowed his love to bring me hope?

_____

_____

_____

_____

Do I believe that God is with me in sorrow, or do I shut him out when I am hurting?

_____

_____

_____

_____

Have I accepted God's gift of hope in the midst of my suffering, or have I rejected it because I was angry or hurt that life wasn't going according to my plans?

_____

_____

_____

_____

Have I shared comfort with others in my life? How can I do that now?

_____

_____

_____

_____

How can I bind the wounds of others, sharing with them the healing and grace Christ has given to me?

_____

_____

_____

_____

WEEK 5

LET'S BE HONEST . . .

There are six things which the LORD hates,
seven which are an abomination to him:
haughty eyes, a lying tongue,
and hands that shed innocent blood,
a heart that devises wicked plans,
feet that make haste to run to evil,
a false witness who breathes out lies,
and a man who sows discord among brothers.

Proverbs 6:16–19

Probably most of us have heard the phrase "Honesty is the best policy." But that virtue is a difficult one to live out. We don't see it as often as we would like in the world around us, and even in our own lives, many of us struggle sometimes with honesty. Yet, for us as Catholic men, integrity must be foundational to the legacy we leave behind and the inheritance our life is seeking. It is the cement that holds our relationships together, the foundation of every act of love that points the way to the Kingdom of God. How can we take up our cross and follow Jesus, making our mark on the Church, if we are not willing to be honest about who we are, where we are going, and how we serve?

When we abandon integrity, we lose touch with our identity as Catholic men. Everything in our lives is thrown out of sync. We begin traveling down a dark path where sinful thoughts lead to wrong actions, which sow discord within the Body of Christ. This slippery slope, where the first falsehood leads to rationalization and more lies, dishonors our birthright as Catholics and serves as a poor testimony of the grace that has transformed our lives. But as we live honest lives, we shape the future of the Church into the image of the Savior, who came to bring us the truth.

This week, as we consider the impact integrity has on the legacy we leave behind us, we will reflect on these truths from Scripture:

1. A blameless life keeps us safe.

"He who walks in integrity will be delivered, / but he who is perverse in his ways will fall into a pit" (Prv 28:18). Honesty carries us through trials and temptations, keeping us from stumbling and falling over our own lies. It allows us to complete our journeys and add our unique spirit to the life of the Church.

2. Honesty is a good and prosperous guide.

"The integrity of the upright guides them, / but the crookedness of the treacherous destroys them" (Prv 11:3). Honesty is single-minded purpose, a faithful roadmap to heaven. Those who seek truth and to be truthful provide a sure and steady lesson of righteousness for those who will come after. By contrast, those who reject honesty become conflicted, double-minded, and confused about which way will lead them home.

3. Our new self has no need for falsehood.

"Do not lie to one another, seeing that you have put off the old man with his practices and have put on the new man, who is being renewed in knowledge after the image of his creator" (Col 3:9–10). We who live in Christ are truly new men. Our lives of integrity shape us ever more closely to the purity of God's image, leaving Christ's holy fingerprint on everything we say and do. New men build up the Church and model the path that future generations are to take.

4. Honest relationships go hand in hand with membership in the Body.

"Therefore, putting away falsehood, let every one speak the truth with his neighbor, for we are members one of another" (Eph 4:25). Honesty builds trust among the members of the Church. We must put off the lies and speak with transparency in order to connect more deeply with our family of faith. These deep and lasting relationships connect us not only to one another but to the entire story of salvation from the Garden of Eden to the New Jerusalem on the Last Day.

5. Integrity is a satisfactory sacrifice that pleases God.

"To do righteousness and justice / is more acceptable to the LORD than sacrifice" (Prv 21:3). We could do a thousand good deeds and give up all we own, but without a deep, honest, loving commitment to integrity, those works will never matter. True righteous living gives meaning to our acts of love, tying them to the sacrifice of Christ through the lives we offer to God in faith.

This Week's Call to Action

Honesty is a lifelong discipline; and the more we live in the truth, the deeper it grows. The world is watching us to see if we are truly living out what we say we believe. An honest Catholic man is a powerful witness in a world where dishonesty and falsehood are everywhere. A life of integrity leaves a lasting impression upon the body of believers and upon those who are searching for a Savior as well. Truth sheds light upon the darkness of this world and draws men and women toward the eternal inheritance that awaits all who pledge their lives to Christ.

This week, strive to be more consciously aware of your words and actions as you endeavor to be a man of truth and integrity. Hold yourself accountable for every little temptation to "stretch the truth," and take seriously your call to be a man of truth and a pillar of strength through your honest example to those around you. Think of ways you can build up the Body of Christ by living as an honest man. Consider what changes might have to take place in your life in order for you to be a man of integrity who puts the Gospel, the Body of Christ, and the will of Almighty God first in your life.

SUNDAY

This week we will reflect on what it means to be a man of honesty and integrity, living a blameless life that is pleasing to God. Being blameless keeps us safe, brings inner prosperity, and goes hand in hand with being a member of the Body of Christ. Through Christ, each of us has been made a new creature, free to live a life of righteousness. Christ calls us to work out our salvation by the grace-inspired, grace-enabled power of God that is poured out into our lives every day through prayer, the sacraments, and fellowship with other believers.

As you celebrate the Eucharist this week, consider how our worship is so bound to the eternal, once-for-all sacrifice of Christ on the cross. Meditate on how the integrity of the Mass shapes us to live lives of sacrifice and praise. In your prayer (and in your journal if you choose to write), take an honest inventory of your heart, considering some of the ways you have failed to be a man of integrity. Come up with practical solutions to help you to overcome your struggles and live a more honest life for Jesus. List the lies that the world tells you and speak the truth against them, developing practical steps you will take to live out the transformed life that is yours in Christ.

Questions for reflection
Ask yourself honestly: Am I living as a man of integrity?

LET'S BE HONEST . . .   73

Who in your life provides an example of honesty and integrity in the face of the dishonesty of the world?

How can you speak truth into the life of a brother this week?

Praying with Scripture

"Do your best to present yourself to God as one approved, a workman who has no need to be ashamed, rightly handling the word of truth" (2 Tm 2:15).

MONDAY
A BLAMELESS LIFE KEEPS US SAFE

Keep your heart with all vigilance;
*   for from it flow the springs of life.*
Put away from you crooked speech,
*   and put devious talk far from you.*
Let your eyes look directly forward,
*   and your gaze be straight before you.*
Take heed to the path of your feet,
*   then all your ways will be sure.*
Do not swerve to the right or to the left;
*   turn your foot away from evil.*

Proverbs 4:23–27

It is frightening to consider just how quickly our lives can spiral out of control when we stray from the path God has laid out for us. Scripture calls us to walk the way of integrity so that we may remain steadfast and safe in all we do. We must hold on to God's teachings, locking them safely in our hearts, keeping them ever ready on our lips, and never letting them out of our sight. A life of truth, grounded on the word of God, guards our hearts, gives us health, and guides our steps as we strive to leave our imprint upon the world. When we stray from the narrow path, we stumble and fall.

Catholic men need to be men of integrity above all other concerns. God's truth must be so embedded in our hearts that our every word breathes life, and our every action builds up. We must be models of righteousness, reliable witnesses to the reality of the Gospel and the soundness of the Body of Christ. Only then can we be faithful, sacrificial servants who rest secure in God's kingdom and present our lives as living legacies of the goodness of Christ.

Questions for reflection

How serious is your commitment to God's teachings on honesty in speech and action?

When have you seen dishonesty tear down your life or the life of another?

What practical steps can you take this week to grow in integrity and faithfulness to the Gospel?

Praying with Scripture

"He who walks in integrity will be delivered, / but he who is perverse in his ways will fall into a pit" (Prv 28:18).

TUESDAY
HONESTY IS A GOOD AND PROSPEROUS GUIDE

Thus says the LORD,
> *your Redeemer, the Holy One of Israel:*
> *I am the LORD your God, who teaches you to profit,*
> *who leads you in the way you should go.*
O that you had listened to my commandments!
> *Then your peace would have been like a river,*
> *and your righteousness like the waves of the sea;*

your offspring would have been like the sand,
    and your descendants like its grains;
their name would never be cut off
    or destroyed from before me.

Isaiah 48:17–19

There are many who feel that life is too difficult for honesty. Their motto is "Me First" and their method is "Whatever gets me what I want" For Catholics, however, our faith and the future of the Church demand that we lead a life of honesty, following God with integrity of heart. As we listen to and accept God's truth, we experience prosperity, inner peace, freedom from guilt, and the abundance of godliness that guides our steps along the narrow way. Our path to heaven becomes clear and our feet become sure along the road.

A Catholic man who lives a life of truth has all the prosperity he will ever need. It shows in his demeanor, his words, and his actions. Others see us as determined holy tour guides who blaze a trail of truth straight into the Kingdom of God.

Questions for reflection
How has living a more honest life brought you clarity, peace, and inner prosperity?

What men in your life stand out as examples of integrity for you to follow?

How can you help a brother this week, who may be struggling to live a life of freedom and integrity?

Praying with Scripture
"The integrity of the upright guides them, / but the crookedness of the treacherous destroys them" (Prv 11:3).

WEDNESDAY
OUR NEW SELF HAS NO NEED FOR FALSEHOOD

*For if we have been united with him in a death like his, we
shall certainly be united with him in a resurrection like his.
We know that our former man was crucified with him so that
the sinful body might be destroyed, and we might no longer be
enslaved to sin. For he who has died is freed from sin. But if we
have died with Christ, we believe that we shall also live with
him. For we know that Christ being raised from the dead will
never die again; death no longer has dominion over him. The
death he died he died to sin, once for all, but the life he lives he
lives to God. So you also must consider yourselves dead to sin
and alive to God in Christ Jesus.*

Romans 6:5–11

In Christ, we have become new creatures who no longer live by
the ways of falsehood. Through the Holy Spirit, we have power
over the slavery of sin and strength to live out the promises that
are ours by virtue of our membership in the Body of Christ.
We no longer need to carry the sinful man around with us. We
can put him off, and put on Christ, every day of our lives.

Because we have been transformed by Jesus, we are free
to open our lives to all that is good, noble, and just. We can
fill our minds with beauty and goodness. We can choose what
is wonderful over what is unworthy, and seek to live a life of
excellence and purity. As new men in Christ, we should be a
model for others to follow, drawing everyone we meet to Jesus
through our words and actions. Freed from falsehood, we leave
our indelible mark upon the world, daily revealing our unity
with our risen Lord.

Questions for reflection
Do you live each day as a new man in Christ, free from the
power of sin?

What is one specific way you can grow in integrity and grace in days to come?

How can you walk with a brother who is striving to put off the old man and put on Christ?

Praying with Scripture
"Do not lie to one another, seeing that you have put off the old man with his practices and have put on the new man, who is being renewed in knowledge after the image of his creator" (Col 3:9–10).

THURSDAY
HONEST RELATIONSHIPS GO HAND IN HAND WITH MEMBERSHIP IN THE BODY

I give thanks to God always for you because of the grace of God which was given you in Christ Jesus, that in every way you were enriched in him with all speech and all knowledge — even as the testimony to Christ was confirmed among you — so that you are not lacking in any spiritual gift, as you wait for the revealing of our Lord Jesus Christ; who will sustain you to the end, guiltless in the day of our Lord Jesus Christ. God is faithful, by whom you were called into the fellowship of his Son, Jesus Christ our Lord. I appeal to you, brethren, by the name of our Lord Jesus Christ, that all of you agree and that there be no dissensions among you, but that you be united in the same mind and the same judgment.

1 Corinthians 1:4–10

As members of the Body of Christ, we have a duty to live irreproachably, never bringing harm to the Church or causing scandal. In particular, we are called to honesty in our relationships with one another. Only as we are open and truthful can we make real connections to one another and to Jesus our Head. As humanity awaits the revelation of Jesus Christ, we are called to stand together in unity, helping the Body to growth to maturity.

The legacy we offer to the world will not hold together if our fellowship is marred by insincerity and division. We will not point the way to what is to come if falsehood causes us to focus more on ourselves than on the Body of Christ. In unity is peace, sound judgment, and a purpose grounded on the true knowledge of Jesus and his saving work on the cross. We cannot be lacking in any gift needed to carry the Church to the Second Coming of the Lord.

Questions for reflection

Do you live in complete honesty in your relationships with others, or does dishonesty cloud some of your interactions?

How has dishonesty and lack of integrity wounded your relationships in the past? How does this impact the Body of Christ?

How can you speak a unifying message of truth to a brother who may need to be brought into greater fellowship with the Church?

Praying with Scripture

"Therefore, putting away falsehood, let every one speak the truth with his neighbor, for we are members one of another" (Eph 4:25).

FRIDAY
INTEGRITY IS A SATISFACTORY SACRIFICE THAT PLEASES GOD

O LORD, who shall sojourn in your tent?
Who shall dwell on your holy mountain?
He who walks blamelessly, and does what is right,

and speaks truth from his heart;
who does not slander with his tongue,
and does no evil to his friend,
nor takes up a reproach against his neighbor;
in whose eyes a reprobate is despised,
but who honors those who fear the LORD;
who swears to his own hurt and does not change;
who does not put out his money at interest,
and does not take a bribe against the innocent.
He who does these things shall never be moved.

Psalm 15

All the good deeds we could ever do could never win our way into heaven. Yet, as transformed believers, our lives become a living sacrifice, offered to God in praise and thanksgiving, holy and pleasing in every way. As we walk in integrity, blameless of heart and committed to righteousness, we become immovable and solid. The world cannot shake us, and yet our lives and our legacy can shake the world!

In Jesus, we are graced to live out our faith in the integrity of our good works, offered to the Lord with grateful hearts. We respond to our faith with works of love that are birthed by the grace of the Holy Spirit. Like a memorial carved into solid rock, our lives stand strong to remind the world that it is only in Christ that we can please God, refuse sin, and claim the inheritance that is ours.

Questions for reflection

How does being an immovable man of integrity help you to leave your legacy in the world?

What have you given up to be a more solid believer? What have you gained for yourself and for the Church you serve because of that surrender?

What can you do to become more and more a living sacrifice

to your heavenly Father and a better example to your Catholic brothers?

Praying with Scripture

"To do righteousness and justice / is more acceptable to the LORD than sacrifice" (Prv 21:3).

SATURDAY

Go Deeper

Have I experienced the security and safety of an honest life in Christ? Have I thanked God for the gift of a life lived with integrity?

_____

_____

_____

_____

Where do I need to work on living with integrity? In what ways do I allow dishonesty to creep into my life, whether in word or action?

_____

_____

_____

_____

What habits of thinking, speaking, and acting do I need to put off so that I can more fully put on Christ?

_____

_____

_____

_____

_____

Am I striving to become a living sacrifice, pleasing to God and effective to others? Where have I allowed laziness, selfishness, fear, or something else to keep me from giving fully of myself?

_____

_____

_____

_____

Do I build up the Body of Christ through honest living? How can I walk with my brothers in Christ as they seek to live honest lives of integrity?

_____

_____

_____

_____

WEEK 6

ACCOUNTABILITY PARTNERS

Brethren, if a man is overtaken in any trespass, you who are spiritual should restore him in a spirit of gentleness. Look to yourself, lest you too be tempted. Bear one another's burdens, and so fulfil the law of Christ. For if any one thinks he is something, when he is nothing, he deceives himself. But let each one test his own work, and then his reason to boast will be in himself alone and not in his neighbor. For each man will have to bear his own load.

Galatians 6:1–5

One of the hardest roles a Catholic man may face is to walk beside a brother who has strayed from the narrow path. It is not easy to confront sin or to correct the sinner. Neither is it easy to be confronted or corrected when we have done wrong. Such confrontation always puts us at risk for reprimand, ridicule, and rejection. Yet we are responsible for one another, and to the Church as a whole. Part of leaving a lasting legacy of faith is rooting out sin and lifting up our brothers as together we walk the path toward perfection.

Tension within the Body of Christ is never easy to face, but it should not keep us from working to restore our relationships and draw one another closer to Christ. So how does a Catholic man confront his brother in order to turn him from his sin? How does accountability help us to be men who point the way to our inheritance in heaven? This week, we will consider the following ideas:

1. Truth is crucial, but gentleness is key.

While we must respond to sin from a perspective of justice, we need to do so in a way that is caring and kind. "Speaking the truth in love" (Eph 4:15) should be our foundational guide as we approach our brother about his sin.

2. We must bear each other's burdens for the sake of love.

We cannot confront sin without loving the sinner. We must walk alongside our brother, bearing the burden as a member of the Body, for when one part suffers, all the members suffer as well (cf. 1 Cor 12:26).

3. We need to be careful that we ourselves do not fall.

Pride, arrogance, and overconfidence in our abilities can lead us into the same sins that we point out in our brothers' lives (cf. 1 Cor 10:12). We must be willing to hear correction from our brothers, thank them for it, and then act on what we hear. Though we bear one another's burdens, we are responsible for our own sins.

4. Transparency, confession, and forgiveness lead to a stronger Body.

As we share our failings honestly and pray for healing (cf. Jas 5:16), we receive power from the Holy Spirit to unite us and restore us as a family of faith. As we forgive, we grow stronger as a Church.

5. Compassion carries on the saving power of the cross.

We are called to show kindness and compassion to one another, forgiving as we have been forgiven in Christ (cf. Eph 4:32). The same power that saves us is meant to spread into the Body of Christ and beyond.

This Week's Call to Action

When we look to God's word, the teachings of the Church, and our own experiences of healing as we speak to the issue of sin, we can bring reconciliation and restoration to our brothers. This week, focus on two things: getting real about your own struggles with sin, and considering how you can come alongside your brothers and hold them accountable before God. Let your truth be tempered by tenderness and your wisdom shared with humility as you and your brothers walk the narrow way together. Know that you are saints saved from sin by grace. Be ready to confess your sins to those you have hurt and to make peace for the sake of the Gospel and the building up of the Body.

Make time to go to confession as well, to receive absolution and grace for the journey. Guard your heart and help your brothers to guard theirs as together you walk the journey of faith. Always remember that there is no room for superiority, for without the grace of Christ we would all fail in our journeys as Catholic men. Confronting sin is more about sharing burdens than preaching repentance. It is more about self-examination and humility than pronouncing judgment on a broken soul.

How we confront sin is as important as why we confront sin. Many of us have experienced the cruel correcting tongue of a self-righteous and superior Christian who felt compelled to point out our sin with a "word from the Lord." That kind of arrogance is a poor witness to the Gospel. It is only when we travel the road to recovery with our brothers that the Gospel can be fully shared and the legacy of our Catholic faith be upheld and carried into the future.

SUNDAY

Our calling to hold one another accountable is a serious one. This week, focus on what it means to confront sin in your family of faith. Such accountability should take place in an atmosphere of gentleness, love, and mutual appreciation for one another. We cannot be complacent believers, but must be disciplined and diligent in order to keep from falling into sin ourselves. This week, seek to connect your own compassion for your brothers to the Church and her mission to grow in unity through the Holy Spirit. As we continue the legacy of the cross in our sacrificial love for one another, we must hold our brothers and ourselves accountable for our good and the good of the Body of Christ.

This Sunday, consider the Mass as an accountability meeting. As you lift up one another in prayer, as you confess your need for Christ, and as you draw near to the table in unity, thank God for the love he has shown you on the cross. In your prayer (and in your journaling, if you choose), consider ways you can continue to hold your brothers accountable. Reflect on your own shortcomings and failings, and thank God for the love that bled and died on the cross.

Questions for reflection
How can you get more in touch with your own walk with Christ, and the areas where he is inviting you to conversion and healing?

How can you confront sin and imperfection in your brothers with gentleness, humility, and honesty?

Praying with Scripture
"My brethren, if any one among you wanders from the truth and some one brings him back, let him know that whoever brings back a sinner from the error of his way will save his soul from death and will cover a multitude of sins" (Jas 5:19–20).

MONDAY
Truth Is Crucial, but Gentleness Is Key

And the Lord's servant must not be quarrelsome but kindly to every one, an apt teacher, forbearing, correcting his opponents with gentleness. God may perhaps grant that they will repent and come to know the truth, and they may escape from the snare of the devil, after being captured by him to do his will.

2 Timothy 2:24–26

Many a man has been lost to sin through the careless words of a self-righteous judge. While it is important to confront a sinner with the truth of his sin, we must do so with a heart that mirrors the compassion of Christ. Rather than trying to win an argument or expose a crime, a Catholic man needs to be gentle, patient, and understanding in challenging his brother about his sin. A man under the influence of the enemy will be defensive and see his situation from a clouded perspective. We must approach him as Our Lord approached so many hurting souls: with gentleness and love.

We must allow the power of the Holy Spirit to change our brother's heart. If we permit arrogance or pride to rule our hearts, our brother will shut down to us and we will accomplish nothing. Ultimately, it is the grace of God that leads a brother to turn away from his sin. The key to true accountability is tying our actions to the overall mission and end of Christianity. When we choose to walk a gentle road with a broken sinner, ever mindful of how our journeys will affect the Church, we open the door for change and yield to the love of God that saves us from ourselves.

Questions for reflection
When have you allowed a judgmental spirit rather than a loving spirit to rule your heart? What was the result?

How have you grown in your ability to respond to sin with gentleness and patience?

When have you seen God work in a brother's life to turn him back to Jesus?

Praying with Scripture

"Rather, speaking the truth in love, we are to grow up in every way into him who is the head, into Christ" (Eph 4:15).

TUESDAY
WE MUST BEAR EACH OTHER'S BURDENS FOR THE SAKE OF LOVE

Is not this the fast that I choose:
  to loose the bonds of wickedness,
  to undo the thongs of the yoke,
to let the oppressed go free,
  and to break every yoke?
Is it not to share your bread with the hungry,
  and bring the homeless poor into your house;
when you see the naked, to cover him,
  and not to hide yourself from your own flesh?
Then shall your light break forth like the dawn,
  and your healing shall spring up speedily;
your righteousness shall go before you,
  the glory of the LORD shall be your rear guard.

Isaiah 58:6–8

Many men become so caught up in their sin because they believe that no one cares about them. They feel entitled to the pleasure their sin brings them, holding bitterness or anger in their hearts over how they have been treated in the past. It is no good to confront sin if we do not love the sinner. Jesus never excused sin when he saw it, but he loved those who were guilty of falling into sin and longed to draw them back home to himself.

When we share in the burdens our brothers are bearing, we bring strength into the situation. Sin often manifests itself because of pain, confusion, and bitterness. When we come alongside our brother and join him in bearing the suffering he is undergoing, we shine the light of Christ's love on the path. This allows our brother to see how his walk of faith is connected to the overall good of the Church. When we seek to alleviate our brother's burden and help him take his important place within the Church, he becomes much more likely to surrender his sin to God. As the members of the Body join together in suffering, we pave the way for righteousness and joy to be restored and we build up the Church and her mission to point the lost toward the ultimate goal of heaven.

Questions for reflection

Why do you think sharing in your brother's suffering helps to turn him from his sin? Have you experienced this in your life?

Have you ever looked past a brother's sin to see the pain behind it? What was the result?

What are some practical ways you can come alongside a brother who is trapped in sin and gently draw him back into his role within the Church?

Praying with Scripture

"If one member suffers, all suffer together; if one member is honored, all rejoice together" (1 Cor 12:26).

WEDNESDAY
We Need to Be Careful That We Ourselves Do Not Fall

Therefore let any one who thinks that he stands take heed lest he fall. No temptation has overtaken you that is not common to man. God is faithful, and he will not let you be tempted beyond your strength, but with the temptation will also provide the way of escape, that you may be able to endure it.

1 Corinthians 10:12–13

God's word provides plenty of warning about falling into sin, yet we often fail to see our own sin until it's too late. Falling is never pleasant. It brings embarrassment, confusion, disappointment, and can even lead to despair. God, however, provides a remedy for sin, an escape that is laid out before us, provided we are open and humble enough to take it in faith.

Accountability begins with discerning our own faults and failings. We must remember that without the grace of God we would not be able to stand. Sometimes it can be easier to see the sins and imperfections of our brothers than it is to see our own. Yet we cannot hold our brothers accountable or accompany them on the path to perfection if we are not willing to see our own sins, and our own need for accountability. Our ability to make a positive mark on the Church will fall short unless we are willing to see our own sin before we see our brother's.

Questions for reflection

Have you fallen into sin due to your own arrogance and pride? How did you come to recognize the situation, and what did you do about it?

How do you respond when another person confronts you in some sin or failing? Do you allow your brothers to accompany you and lift you up when you stumble?

How has personal accountability helped you to have a greater impact on others' lives and on the future of the Church?

Praying with Scripture

"Well, I do not run aimlessly, I do not box as one beating the air; but I pommel my body and subdue it, lest after preaching to others I myself should be disqualified" (1 Cor 9:26–27).

THURSDAY
TRANSPARENCY, CONFESSION, AND FORGIVENESS LEAD TO A STRONGER BODY

Is any one among you suffering? Let him pray. Is any cheerful? Let him sing praise. Is any among you sick? Let him call for the elders of the Church, and let them pray over him, anointing him with oil in the name of the Lord; and the prayer of faith will save the sick man, and the Lord will raise him up; and if he has committed sins, he will be forgiven. Therefore confess your sins to one another, and pray for one another, that you may be healed. The prayer of a righteous man has great power in its effects.

James 5:13–16

As members of the Church, we share a wonderful joy in being able to support others when they are sick at heart. Our physical well-being is intimately connected to our spiritual condition. The forgiveness of sin is tied to the alleviation of personal suffering, as the passage above demonstrates. It is a beautiful expression of the fellowship that brings healing to the brethren.

When we open our hearts to one another, confessing our sins and calling out to the Church for healing, we draw upon the power of the Holy Spirit and find restoration and renewal. Just as a right attitude and a healed heart can influence the healing of our physical body, so too can confession and forgiveness among Church members help to bring greater unity and healing to the Body of Christ. It is part of what it means to leave our legacy within the Church. Unity and reconciliation build up the members and carry out the eternal mission of Christianity.

Questions for reflection
Have you experienced healing and strength in the sacraments of the Church? How?

Have you seen the impact your own personal healing has had on the Body of Christ? What has that been like?

How can you help to bring healing to a brother in Christ?

Praying with Scripture
"Finally, all of you, have unity of spirit, sympathy, love of the brethren, a tender heart and a humble mind" (1 Pt 3:8).

FRIDAY
COMPASSION CARRIES ON THE SAVING POWER OF THE CROSS

He himself bore our sins in his body on the tree, that we might die to sin and live to righteousness. By his wounds you have been healed. For you were straying like sheep, but have now returned to the Shepherd and Guardian of your souls.

1 Peter 2:24–25

Blessed be the God and Father of our Lord Jesus Christ, the Father of mercies and God of all comfort, who comforts us in all our affliction, so that we may be able to comfort those who are in any affliction, with the comfort with which we ourselves are comforted by God.

2 Corinthians 1:3–4

Our compassion to one another is an extension of the sacrifice of Jesus on the cross — the same sacrifice we experience and in which we participate each time we attend Mass. We are living out the love that poured forth from the heart of the Son of God to all humanity. The power that saved the straying sheep of the flock of God continues to save through the Church. As we show compassion, kindness, and comfort to the family of faith, we continue the legacy of the cross and its power to save lost souls.

The One who bore our sins reveals himself to us through the word, the sacraments, and the members of the Body who carry the message of the cross into their everyday lives. Each day we live out the mission of Christ to bring the lost back into the fold of God by all we say and do. What a powerful privilege and sobering responsibility we have to carry on the love of Christ expressed so perfectly in his sacrificial death on the cross!

Questions for reflection
Have you experienced the joy of helping a brother return to the Church? Have you made such a journey yourself? Who accompanied you?

When you participate in the Mass, do you recognize that you are truly present at the foot of the cross? The next time you attend Mass, how can you reflect on this profound truth and pray for the grace to enter in more deeply?

How can you extend the healing and saving power of the cross to your brothers?

Praying with Scripture
"And be kind to one another, tenderhearted, forgiving one another, as God in Christ forgave you" (Eph 4:32).

SATURDAY

Go Deeper

Have I confronted sin and imperfection in my brothers with gentleness and humility, or have I neglected this calling or carried it out with arrogance and anger?

_____

_____

_____

_____

Have I neglected to guard my own mind and heart and fallen into any sinful habits?

_____

_____

_____

_____

Have I accepted correction from another with humility and gratitude, or did I respond in anger and defensiveness?

_____

_____

_____

Have I gone to confession recently? Do I encourage others to partake of this sacrament?

_____

_____

_____

_____

How can I help to make the sacrifice of Christ on the cross a more visible reality in the world around me?

_____

_____

_____

_____

Do I have an accountability partner in my walk with Christ? If not, who in my life could fill that role? Am I willing to ask him? Am I an accountability partner to others?

_____

_____

_____

_____

_____

WEEK 7

Do Not Fret!

Take delight in the LORD,
*   and he will give you the desires of your heart.*
Commit your way to the LORD;
*   trust in him, and he will act.*
He will bring forth your vindication as the light,
*   and your right as the noonday.*
Be still before the LORD, and wait patiently for him;
*   do not fret over him who prospers in his way,*
*   over the man who carries out evil devices!*
Refrain from anger, and forsake wrath!
*   Do not fret; it tends only to evil.*
For the wicked shall be cut off;
*   but those who wait for the LORD shall possess the land.*

Psalm 37:4–9

The world can seem like an overwhelming place. We try to live in peace with others and find meaning in what we do, but often it seems as though the enemy of our souls is winning the battle. As we seek to leave a legacy of faith, we are often confronted by fear and doubt. God, however, offers us another way. He sees the end from the beginning and has control over all things. He knows the plans he has for us, and they are hopeful and good (cf. Jer 29:11).

We may be tempted to give in to our fears and surrender the fight, but God calls us to put our trust in him, to respond to fear with faith and to the storms of life with strength. As we surrender to the will of our loving God, we are lifted above the troubles of this life and see our situation through the lens of God's perfect plan. God's will becomes clear, and we take hold of our eternal inheritance. This heavenly vision shapes how we live our lives and the meaningful mark we seek to leave upon the world.

This week we will focus on how we as men can take hold of the eternal gifts that are ours as we put worry in its proper place. We will replace fear with God's truth and allow it to teach us how to live the life of a man of legacy.

1. Taking on God's eternal perspective frees us from worry.

While we have much in our lives that causes us to worry, this condition is temporary. Thanks to Christ's sacrifice on the cross, we now possess an eternal legacy. We can lay down our worries at the foot of the cross and carry on in hope, writing the story of our lives through the power of the Holy Spirit.

2. Trust triumphs over doubt and fear.

Our security depends not on our own efforts, but on the loving care of our Savior. As we surrender to God's care, we settle into the role God has set up for us. In faith, we offer our lives as a testimony of the salvation story of Christ.

3. Our days should be filled with joy.

As we come to dwell in the shadow of God's protection, we find an inexpressible joy that cannot be snuffed out by the struggles of life. Joy is strength that provides purpose and guides the way we live our lives and leave our mark on the world.

4. As we trust, we become shining stars.

With God's light to support us, we become powerful witnesses to the world. In the midst of all their worries and struggles, others will be able to see in us the face of God, who loves us through our trials. Our lives become living examples of Christ's love, perfect pictures of the grace that flows freely into the lives of all who come seeking the inheritance of heaven.

5. Those who are protected cannot be provoked.

The world will try to push us into anger and retaliation, yet when we rely on God's sovereign protection, we have the strength to respond with love and patience. We cast aside worry and replace it with trust because we are at rest in the embrace of our loving God. We become a portrait of grace that shines like a beacon leading those who come after us straight into the Kingdom of God.

This Week's Call to Action

Being a Catholic man means the world does not have to have its way in your life. As you move through this week, spend time resting in the arms of your almighty, loving Creator, laying your cares and worries before him. Work this week to fill your heart with joy and continue to trust the God who works all things out to the good (cf. Rom 8:28). Seek out other men who can provide good counsel and support as you face your worries and concerns. Support your brothers with prayer and acts of love in their own worries as well.

Meditate on the kind of legacy you want to leave the Body of Christ. Let your faith guide your understanding of what it means to live in total trust, casting aside fear in favor of hope. Consider how your ultimate vision of heaven should shape the way you live. Think of ways you can express your legacy goals to others as you strive to make your mark on the world.

SUNDAY

This week, focus on how you can avoid the pitfalls of worry. Strive to look at your own weaknesses in light of Christ's eternal strength. Meditate on trust, which overcomes fear and doubt and helps you to fill your days with joy. As you allow God's grace to lift you from your worries, consider how you can become a shining light for others, rather than letting anyone provoke you to the point of falling into fear.

At Mass this week, pay special attention to the prayers of petition, especially the Prayer of the Faithful. Let trust motivate you to give yourself fully over to worship, praying in confidence for God's strength and celebrating that the greatest gift he has given us is our salvation in Christ. Consider how the Mass strengthens you to walk each day in delight and joy, moving forward with hope. In prayer, place before God any doubts and fears that may be troubling you. Thank God for the people and events that have come into your life to help you conquer worry and replace it with faith.

Questions for reflection

What worries in your life do you need to surrender to God's perfect, loving care?

This week, how will you make time to strengthen your faith through times of prayer, study, and fellowship with other Catholic men?

Praying with Scripture

"Have no anxiety about anything, but in everything by prayer and supplication with thanksgiving let your requests be made known to God. And the peace of God, which passes all understanding, will keep your hearts and your minds in Christ Jesus" (Phil 4:6–7).

MONDAY
TAKING ON GOD'S ETERNAL PERSPECTIVE FREES US FROM WORRY

You have been born anew, not of perishable seed but of imper-
ishable, through the living and abiding word of God; for
  "All flesh is like grass
  and all its glory like the flower of grass.
  The grass withers, and the flower falls,
  but the word of the Lord abides for ever."
That word is the good news which was preached to you.

1 Peter 1:23–25

Human beings often believe that we matter much more than we do. Yet in comparison with our all-powerful, all-knowing, everlasting Father, we are a vapor that appears for a little while and then vanishes away (cf. Jas 4:14). In Jesus Christ, the Lamb led to slaughter to redeem us from our sins, we have been given new eyes to see our position as it really is. Kingdoms rise up and fade away. Men of power eventually come to nothing. The only true lasting legacies are those centered on the Gospel of love.

Because we have this eternal perspective, we are called to live without anxiety or worry, confident that God will give us all we need to reach heaven. Though our flesh is like the fading glory of a flower, in Christ we are now made of imperishable material — never to fade, destined for unity, glory, peace, and joy with God in heaven for all eternity.

Questions for reflection
Have you ever experienced just how small and fragile your life is compared to God? What was that like?

Does maintaining an eternal perspective on your life and legacy free you from worry? How?

How can you help a brother in Christ remember God's eternal care in the face of his worries and concerns?

Praying with Scripture
"LORD, let me know my end, / and what is the measure of my days; / let me know how fleeting my life is!" (Ps 39:4).

TUESDAY
TRUST TRIUMPHS OVER DOUBT AND FEAR

Behold, the eye of the LORD is on those who fear him,
*   on those who hope in his merciful love,*
that he may deliver their soul from death,
*   and keep them alive in famine.*
Our soul waits for the LORD;
*   he is our help and shield.*
Yes, our heart is glad in him,
*   because we trust in his holy name.*
Let your mercy, O LORD, be upon us,
*   even as we hope in you.*

Psalm 33:18–22

There are certainly times when we look to the heavens and wonder if God really cares about the people he made. Sometimes it can seem easier to believe in an all-powerful God than to believe that he is concerned for us. Yet for us as Catholics, that anxiety has been shattered by the cross. We no longer have to worry about whether God loves us. He has shown us that he does by giving his only Son for the salvation of our souls.

Additionally, we can be assured that all the worries we face are under God's sovereign control. God watches over us and delivers us through his strength. He knows what we need and works all things out in accordance with his perfect, holy will.

Our future in heaven is assured, our legacy on earth is secure. We demonstrate our patience as we wait for our deliverance and speak Christ's holy name with confidence to the People of God. No matter what we are going through at any moment, our Father is looking down on us, covering us with his steadfast love and singing his eternal song in our hearts.

Questions for reflection

Have you ever experienced circumstances that caused you to question God's will for your life? What was it like?

Has there been a time in your life when you turned to the feeble strength of this world rather than God's perfect love in the face of some doubt or worry? What was the result?

When have you seen your Father's watchful care bring you victory and peace?

Praying with Scripture

"The Lord is my strength and my song, / and he has become my salvation; / this is my God, and I will praise him, / my father's God, and I will exalt him" (Ex 15:2).

WEDNESDAY
OUR DAYS SHOULD BE FILLED WITH JOY

Though the fig tree does not blossom,
nor fruit be on the vines,
the produce of the olive fail
and the fields yield no food,
the flock be cut off from the fold
and there be no herd in the stalls,
yet I will rejoice in the LORD,
I will joy in the God of my salvation.

GOD, *the Lord, is my strength;*
  he makes my feet like deer's feet,
  he makes me tread upon my high places.

Habakkuk 3:17–19

Experience has shown us that the circumstances of our lives
can change in an instant. A car or necessary appliance breaks
down, or a job ends and money becomes tight. A sudden illness
or untimely death brings pain and sorrow we never thought we
would face. The mountains of life stand before us as seemingly
immovable obstacles. In such times, it can be easy to despair.
For believers, however, even in the tough times, we can hold
on to joy.

Because we are covered by God's perfect love, we can place
all our troubles at his feet. He gives us the strength to rejoice
in our legacy of salvation, making our steps steady and sure so
that we can journey to heaven with great joy and fullness of
heart. We have been transformed by the cross and made into
new creatures, full of the expectation of the glories that are
to come. This gives us the freedom to live in joy and peace
even when circumstances are bleak and difficult. Even when
joy seems elusive, we know we have the grace and the freedom
to choose it.

Questions for reflection

How has Jesus revealed his love to you in the midst of struggle
and loss?

Have you experienced joy and peace in the midst of suffering?
What was that experience like?

How can you share the delight of God's presence with a brother who is struggling today?

Praying with Scripture

"You show me the path of life; / in your presence there is fulness of joy, / in your right hand are pleasures for evermore" (Ps 16:11).

THURSDAY
As We Trust, We Become Shining Stars

You are the light of the world. A city set on a hill cannot be hidden. Nor do men light a lamp and put it under a bushel, but on a stand, and it gives light to all in the house. Let your light so shine before men, that they may see your good works and give glory to your Father who is in heaven.

Matthew 5:14–16

As we learn to put our trust in Jesus, we need to let our light shine before the whole world. Worry and anxiety are all around us, and many people stumble in darkness, far from hope. Those of us who have the light of Christ cannot hide our light for fear of being ridiculed or ostracized. We have a duty to share the radiance of Christ so that the lost can see the path to heaven and be saved.

Our every word and deed should reflect what Jesus has done for us. As we lay our worries at the Lord's feet, we must put aside doubt, fear, complaints, and selfishness so that we stand out as blameless men in this crooked generation. This is truly what leaving a legacy is all about. When people look at our lives, the truth, passion, and joy of Christ shine so brightly for them that they are bathed in its radiance and moved to seek the greater light.

Questions for reflection
Have you ever kept your light hidden because you feared what people might think or say? What was the result?

How does trusting God allow your light to shine within the Church and the world?

What do you think others see when they observe how you live your life as a Catholic man?

Praying with Scripture

"For once you were darkness, but now you are light in the Lord; walk as children of light (for the fruit of light is found in all that is good and right and true)" (Eph 5:8–9).

FRIDAY
THOSE WHO ARE PROTECTED CANNOT BE PROVOKED

Praise the LORD!
Blessed is the man who fears the LORD,
who greatly delights in his commandments!
His descendants will be mighty in the land;
the generation of the upright will be blessed.
Wealth and riches are in his house;
and his righteousness endures for ever.
Light rises in the darkness for the upright;
the LORD is gracious, merciful, and righteous.
It is well with the man who deals generously and lends,
who conducts his affairs with justice.
For the righteous will never be moved;
he will be remembered for ever.

Psalm 112:1–6

It is a sad reality that those who believe in Jesus will face hatred and persecution from the world. It may come from coworkers or family members or unbelievers who are hostile to what Jesus offers. Many will try to point out the flaws in our beliefs or our character, call us hypocrites, or challenge our morality, in order to justify their own twisted view of the world. How Catholic men respond to this provocation is critically important.

Men who are grounded in the Gospel, whose eyes are fixed

on the Lord, will not let our trust be shaken by the ridicule of the world. We will persevere in our faith, delighting in the law of love and conducting our affairs with justice and integrity. It is at times of oppression that our legacy is truly fashioned into something that will stand strong until the end. In the fires of persecution, our holy birthright becomes the most potent and powerful for changing lives and building up the Church.

Questions for reflection
What circumstances have helped to temper and refine the legacy you are leaving behind?

How do you answer those who try to tell you your faith is a vain hope?

How can you help a brother stand firm against the ridicule and rejection of the world?

Praying with Scripture
"The righteous will never be removed, / but the wicked will not dwell in the land" (Prv 10:30).

SATURDAY

Go Deeper
Have I allowed worry, anxiety, or fear to turn me away from God's providence and care? What worries do I need to lay at his feet?

How has God's strength helped me overcome fear or anxiety in my life? How has it helped me this week? Have I thanked him?

_____

_____

_____

_____

Do I allow others to help me stay focused on Christ when I am tempted to worry, or do I try to get through it with my own strength?

_____

_____

_____

_____

Who in my life allows the light of Christ to shine through? How can I follow this example of trust in God?

_____

_____

_____

_____

_____

Do I support my brothers in their doubts? How can I be more proactive about helping others who are facing anxiety or struggling to trust God?

_____

_____

_____

_____

WEEK 8

SHOES OF THE FISHERMAN

Now when Jesus came into the district of Caesarea Philippi, he asked his disciples, "Who do men say that the Son of man is?" And they said, "Some say John the Baptist, others say Elijah, and others Jeremiah or one of the prophets." He said to them, "But who do you say that I am?" Simon Peter replied, "You are the Christ, the Son of the living God." And Jesus answered him, "Blessed are you, Simon Bar-Jona! For flesh and blood has not revealed this to you, but my Father who is in heaven. And I tell you, you are Peter, and on this rock I will build my Church, and the gates of Hades shall not prevail against it. I will give you the keys of the kingdom of heaven, and whatever you bind on earth shall be bound in heaven, and whatever you loose on earth shall be loosed in heaven."

Matthew 16:13–19

The Catholic Church teaches that Jesus placed the care of his Church into the hands of his twelve Apostles, giving Peter the primacy as the "rock" upon which he built his Church. Jesus even changed his name from Simon to Peter (which means "rock"). Peter was a man of faith, whose proclamation that Jesus was the Christ was breathed into him by God. Jesus, in turn, blessed Peter with the promise that he would receive the authority to lead the Church after Jesus ascended to heaven.

Peter, the other Apostles, and all their successors have been called to assume the role of shepherding the Church.

Jesus chose to place the task of leading the Church on earth into the hands of Peter and all who would follow in the shoes of this humble fisherman. Through the Holy Spirit, the leaders of the Church have been gifted to guide the Church into all truth. As Catholics, we can be assured that the Church will never falter in her call to leave a lasting legacy for the People of God. We can confidently follow the leadership of the Church, knowing that, despite the frailties of human beings and the evils in the world, the People of God will grow to maturity as we prepare for the Second Coming of Christ.

What can Catholic men learn from the example of Peter and all who have had to fill his shoes? How can we join in the legacy of the Church throughout history by following the guidance of her leaders and helping to shape the thing that has so wonderfully shaped us? This week, we will reflect on five key concepts.

1. The Church speaks the truth about Christ.

The Catholic Church has consistently proclaimed important truths about Jesus from the very beginning. The Catholic Church alone has maintained her legacy of truth without compromise. Catholic men can follow and move within the Church to contribute to her future as well.

2. Through the Holy Spirit, the leaders of the Church continue in truth.

Though the Church has always suffered from the sins of her frail human members, including those in positions of leadership within the Church, the Holy Spirit always keeps her alive and brings her through her trials. We can trust that he will always care for the Church and protect her, no matter what evils assail her, until the end of time.

3. The Church today carries on the legacy of the Apostles.

The pope and bishops today carry on the leadership of Christ's

Church in a direct line of succession from the Apostles. Christ built his Church firmly on Peter, the Rock, and promised that the gates of hell will not prevail against it. We journey forward in hope, trusting that God himself has established this system of leadership.

4. Hell will not prove stronger than the Church.

As she journeys to the end of time and Christ's Second Coming, the Church stands firm against the gates of hell, which hold men's souls in prison. The humble, spiritual leadership of the Catholic Church rescues the lost from sin. In the end, she will win the battle for the Kingdom of God.

5. The Church has the keys to the kingdom.

The leadership of the Church has been given the authority to bind and loose, to proclaim truth and refute error, to care for the poor, and to challenge all nations to come to Christ. Because Catholic men share a place in the Body of Christ, they have the responsibility to build a legacy that follows the teachings of the Church while reflecting the individual gifting of each one of us who contributes to the Church's future.

This Week's Call to Action

The same Holy Spirit that moves in the Holy Father, and in every priest within the Church, moves also in the heart of every Catholic man. This week, consider two important things we learn from Peter's proclamation of faith:

> 1) We can trust the Holy Spirit, through her leaders, to guide the Church into all truth.
> 2) All men are called to live out our lives in humble service to the Church and the world, knowing we share in this awesome responsibility.

As we submit to the authority of the Church, we give witness to the power and authority behind all that we do as servants of the Gospel. Consider specific ways you can serve the Church as you honor the Pope and the leaders of the Church, who follow in the footsteps of the Apostles, who followed the Master from the very start.

Recall also that we are called to help shape the very Church that has shaped us. This week, reflect on how you can work for the kingdom by using the gifts you have been given by the Holy Spirit for building up the Body of Christ. Remember that the legacy you leave must be grounded in the doctrines and authority of the Church.

<hr>

SUNDAY

The focus of this week's study is on the authority given to the Church and her leaders, particularly the Holy Father, to help her carry out the call of Christ to spread the Gospel to the world. The Catholic Church has overcome her trials and struggles throughout history, and she continues to grow and mature in the truth. The Holy Spirit is always guiding the Body of Christ, ultimately overcoming the imperfections of her human leaders and bringing truth and healing to bear over and over again. The Church has experienced the failure of many leaders and suffered from many scandals, yet we can rely on Christ's promise that the gates of hell will never prevail against the Catholic Church.

As members of the Church, we have the duty and the privilege to break down the gates of hell and reach out to the lost in the name of Jesus. Each of us must discern how we can serve the Church in her mission and her journey toward heaven.

As you celebrate the Eucharist this Sunday, consider how the structure of the Mass has grown from its primitive form to what it is today. Think about how, although there have been changes in the structure of our worship, the essence of the Mass has not changed since the beginning. Take time to pray for the

Holy Father, your bishop, your parish priests, and all those who lead the Church with the authority of Christ. Think, pray, and (if you are inclined) journal honestly about any struggles you have had with the Church and her leadership, and how you have worked to reconcile with the Body of Christ. Consider where you see the Church heading and how you can use your gifts in service to the Church to help to build a lasting legacy and point the way to the Kingdom of God that is to come.

Questions for reflection
How can you increase your knowledge of the Church and the office of the bishop, especially the pope?

How will you work to spread the Gospel and the teachings of the Church to all those around you?

Praying with Scripture
"He said to him the third time, 'Simon, son of John, do you love me?' Peter was grieved because he said to him the third time, 'Do you love me?' And he said to him, 'Lord, you know everything; you know that I love you.' Jesus said to him, 'Feed my sheep'" (Jn 21:17).

MONDAY
THE CHURCH SPEAKS THE TRUTH ABOUT CHRIST

Only let your manner of life be worthy of the gospel of Christ, so that whether I come and see you or am absent, I may hear of you that you stand firm in one spirit, with one mind striving side by side for the faith of the gospel, and not frightened in anything by your opponents. This is a clear omen to them of their destruction, but of your salvation, and that from God. For it has been granted to you that for the sake of Christ you should not only believe in him but also suffer for his sake, engaged in the same conflict which you saw and now hear to be mine.

Philippians 1:27–30

The Church is not some cultural club for organizing and enacting administrative and spiritual tasks; she is the Mystical Body of Christ, formed under the leadership of the Apostles, guided by the Holy Spirit, and strengthened by the word and the sacraments. She is a living entity, whose members are joined to Christ the Head. We as members of the Church are charged with standing firm in unity, contending with those who would challenge the truth of Jesus Christ.

Together, we are called to take up our cross and follow in the footsteps of Our Lord (cf. Mt 16:24). We have been granted not just to believe, but to share in the sufferings of Christ for the sake of the kingdom. Under the leadership of the pope, the successor of Peter, we are united in doctrine, in spirit, and in purpose, as we journey ever forward in service to one another and the world until Christ comes again. Each of us contributes to the mission of the Church and the call to lead future generations into the kingdom. As we work with our leaders to help shape the Body of Christ, we build a lasting legacy that submits to God's great truths revealed by Christ.

Questions for reflection

Why is it necessary for the Church to be united under her leaders? What role do you play in this?

Have you ever found it difficult to accept the leadership of the pope or other members of the clergy? How have you dealt with these struggles?

How can Catholics engage in honest dialogue with one another over struggles within the Church, while continuing to honor both her leaders and her people?

Praying with Scripture

"If I am delayed, you may know how one ought to behave in the household of God, which is the Church of the living God, the pillar and bulwark of the truth" (1 Tm 3:15).

TUESDAY
THROUGH THE HOLY SPIRIT, THE LEADERS OF THE CHURCH CONTINUE IN TRUTH

I charge you in the presence of God and of Christ Jesus who is to judge the living and the dead, and by his appearing and his kingdom: preach the word, be urgent in season and out of season, convince, rebuke, and exhort, be unfailing in patience and in teaching. For the time is coming when people will not endure sound teaching, but having itching ears they will accumulate for themselves teachers to suit their own likings, and will turn away from listening to the truth and wander into myths. As for you, always be steady, endure suffering, do the work of an evangelist, fulfil your ministry.

2 Timothy 4:1-5

Jesus came to reconcile us to God and to one another, tearing down the dividing wall between Jews and Gentiles by creating one Church united in one Spirit, giving us access to the Father. Jesus built his Church on the foundation of the twelve Apostles, with Peter as the head. Every bishop and pope throughout history has carried on in a direct line of succession from Christ's hand-picked Apostles.

Since the beginning, the Church has seen difficult times, persecution, corruption, and scandal. Some of the men who have led the Church have gone against the will of God and followed their own selfish plans. Still, the Church has withstood these trials, and through the Holy Spirit she has grown and matured, spiritual brick by spiritual brick. Through holy men and women following the example of Jesus, the Church has survived and continued in the truth. Our call is to be holy men of God who follow the leadership of the Church and help guide her into the future.

Questions for reflection

How do you react in the face of scandal and challenging times within the Church?

How are you responding to your call to help build up the Church, under the leadership of the Apostles' successors?

How do you support others in the Church when they struggle with doubts about authority within the Church?

Praying with Scripture

"But you are a chosen race, a royal priesthood, a holy nation, God's own people, that you may declare the wonderful deeds of him who called you out of darkness into his marvelous light" (1 Pt 2:9).

WEDNESDAY
THE CHURCH TODAY CARRIES ON THE LEGACY OF THE APOSTLES

The apostles and the elders were gathered together to consider this matter. And after there had been much debate, Peter rose and said to them, "Brethren, you know that in the early days God made choice among you, that by my mouth the Gentiles should hear the word of the gospel and believe." After they finished speaking, James replied, "Brethren, listen to me. Symeon has related how God first visited the Gentiles, to take out of them a people for his name. Therefore my judgment is that we should not trouble those of the Gentiles who turn to God, but should write to them to abstain from the pollutions of idols and from unchastity and from what is strangled and from blood. For from early generations Moses has had in every city those who preach him, for he is read every sabbath in the synagogues." Then it seemed good to the apostles and the elders, with the whole Church, to choose men from among them and send them to Antioch with Paul and Barnabas. They sent Judas called Barsabbas, and Silas, leading men among the brethren, with the following letter.

Acts 15:6-7, 13-14, 19-23

The power and authority of the Apostles helped to carry the Church from its infancy through the fires of the first persecutions. The Acts of the Apostles covers the trials the first bishops of the Church faced. In every danger and difficulty, the leaders of the Church came together in faith, sought the guidance of the Holy Spirit, consulted Scripture, and considered the teachings that had come before, in order to make wise decisions for the good of the People of God.

Christ told Peter, the man of faith, that he was the "rock" upon which he would build his Church (cf. Mt 16:18). Today the Church continues to build upon that same rock, the foundation which ultimately rests on Christ. Her legacy stretches from the coming of the Holy Spirit to the Second Coming of Jesus on the Last Day. No struggle, no scandal, and no falsehood will prevent the Church from becoming complete in Christ. Our calling is to continue in the truth by how we live and act within the body of believers.

Questions for reflection

What modern-day challenges do you see the Church facing, and how are today's pope and bishops helping us navigate them?

Do you believe that today's bishops carry on the legacy of the Apostles? How do you see this in the Church today?

How often do you hold up your spiritual leaders in prayer?

Praying with Scripture

"Every one then who hears these words of mine and does them will be like a wise man who built his house upon the rock" (Mt 7:24).

THURSDAY
HELL WILL NOT PROVE STRONGER THAN THE CHURCH

And he said to them, "I saw Satan fall like lightning from heaven. Behold, I have given you authority to tread upon serpents and scorpions, and over all the power of the enemy; and nothing shall hurt you."

Luke 10:18-19

And you, who were dead in trespasses and the uncircumcision of your flesh, God made alive together with him, having forgiven us all our trespasses, having canceled the bond which stood against us with its legal demands; this he set aside, nailing it to the cross. He disarmed the principalities and powers and made a public example of them, triumphing over them in him.

Colossians 2:13-15

It can be tempting to put Jesus and Satan on equal footing when it comes to the battle for the souls of men and women. The truth is, there is no comparison. Christ ranks far above every power, every kingdom, and every authority — period! His greatness, his perfection, and his love have destroyed the power of sin and opened up the gates of heaven for all who believe.

The Church that Jesus founded continually marches into battle against the forces of evil. She is the fullness of the One who fills all things. The authority and power that has been passed down since the time of the Apostles propels the Church forward against the gates of hell, breaking them down and freeing men and women from the grip of Satan's lies. This is the legacy of the Church — that she will always survive, and that we, her members, will one day experience the victory that is ours because of Christ. Our great calling is to carry on that legacy by our devotion to the Church that Jesus founded, and our acts of love that build up the Body in his name.

Questions for reflection
Are you ever tempted to doubt the power of God that is present in the Church? How do you face those doubts?

In what ways do you see the Body of Christ breaking down the gates of hell?

How specifically can you join in the battle to win the hearts of those outside the Church?

Praying with Scripture
"And the devil who had deceived them was thrown into the lake of fire and brimstone where the beast and the false prophet were, and they will be tormented day and night for ever and ever" (Rv 20:10).

FRIDAY
THE CHURCH HAS THE KEYS TO THE KINGDOM

Truly, I say to you, whatever you bind on earth shall be bound in heaven, and whatever you loose on earth shall be loosed in heaven. Again I say to you, if two of you agree on earth about anything they ask, it will be done for them by my Father in heaven. For where two or three are gathered in my name, there am I in the midst of them.

Matthew 18:18–20

Some Christian denominations mock the Catholic Church as an institution, claiming it is acting on the authority of human beings alone rather than looking to Christ. They believe that mere mortals have perverted the cause of Christ with man-made rules rather than Spirit-led living. What so many forget is that Christ gave the keys of the kingdom to Peter and the Apostles, granting them and their successors the authority to carry out God's will through the Church.

This cannot be said too many times: The Church is the Mystical Body of Christ, a living institution that grows and matures because God's Spirit moves in her to will and to act. Christ himself has given her leaders the authority to govern. For more than two thousand years, she has continued to weather the storms of persecution, politics, corruption, and crisis because Jesus has promised to be with her until the end of the age (cf. Mt 28:20). As members of the Body of Christ, we contribute to the growth of the Church and the continuation of this great legacy as we use our gifts for the greater good and the glory of God and await our final victory in Jesus.

Questions for reflection
How does knowing that the Church has the authority of Christ guide how you live your life?

Do you use your gifts in service to the Church and her mission? How can you devote more time and energy to fulfilling this duty?

What do we need to pray for as the Church moves forward in her mission to save the lost?

Praying with Scripture
"Fear not, I am the first and the last, and the living one; I died, and behold I am alive for evermore, and I have the keys of Death and Hades" (Rv 1:17–18).

SATURDAY

Go Deeper

Do I believe that the Church was truly founded by Christ, with Peter as the Rock? How does this belief impact the way I live my Catholic faith?

_____

_____

_____

_____

How has the Holy Spirit led me and led my local church into greater truth? What has been the fruit of this?

_____

_____

_____

_____

Do I pray for my pastor, priests, bishop, the pope, and all those in authority within the Church? How can I commit to pray for them with greater fidelity?

_____

_____

_____

Do I seek to use my God-given gifts in service to the Church? If not, why not? How can I give more generously from what I have been given?

_____

_____

_____

_____

What are some concrete ways I can help my brothers live out their calling to serve the Church?

_____

_____

_____

_____

WEEK 9

ARE YOU ASHAMED OF ME?

And he called to him the multitude with his disciples, and said to them, "If any man would come after me, let him deny himself and take up his cross and follow me. For whoever would save his life will lose it; and whoever loses his life for my sake and the gospel's will save it. For what does it profit a man, to gain the whole world and forfeit his life? For what can a man give in return for his life? For whoever is ashamed of me and of my words in this adulterous and sinful generation, of him will the Son of man also be ashamed, when he comes in the glory of his Father with the holy angels."

Mark 8:34–38

Just as men are called to be leaders in their families, so too are we called to take the lead within our family of faith. We are called to take up our cross and follow without hesitation where our Savior leads. Yet many of us seem to be ashamed of what it means to belong to the Body of Christ. We are afraid to share our faith and reluctant to get involved in ministry in the Church. It calls to mind the old question: "If you were arrested for believing in Jesus, would there be enough evidence to convict you?"

Living our legacy as members of the Church means more than merely participating in the rituals and rites of the Church.

It means committing our minds, our muscle, and our very souls to the cause of Christ. Matthew's Gospel has a chilling word for those who do not stand up for Christ: "So every one who acknowledges me before men, I also will acknowledge before my Father who is in heaven; but whoever denies me before men, I also will deny before my Father who is in heaven" (Mt 10:32–33). Each of us must examine our own conscience in this regard, asking ourselves honestly: *Am I ashamed of Jesus, or do I live openly and proudly as one of his followers?*

This week, we will consider these key truths from this passage of the Gospel of Mark:

1. Deny yourself, take up your cross, and follow Christ.
Jesus speaks in no uncertain terms about what it means to believe in him. We must put ourselves aside in order to accept the trials God will allow as we walk the journey of salvation, trusting God's call no matter where that may lead.

2. It's all opposites.
Too many men put themselves first, but Christ calls us to surrender our lives in order to gain true life. Anyone who tries to hold on to his own life will, in the end, be lost. As Catholics, we must put the Gospel, and not ourselves, first. There is no other way to heaven.

3. There is no comparison in the costs.
We could gain untold wealth, fame, or power, but when heaven and earth pass away, all of that will be lost — and so will we. Yet, when we put Christ first, we gain all the riches of the universe, for we gain the Lord Jesus Christ.

4. If we are ashamed of Christ, he will be ashamed of us.
To imagine Jesus saying he is ashamed of us is a frightening and sobering thought. Consider the image of the lost standing before Jesus as they hear the words, "I never knew you. Depart from me, you evildoers" (Mt 7:23). This should not be.

5. Christ is coming into his glory.

In the end, Jesus Christ will come again to judge the living and the dead. We need to consider just what that will mean for those who reject the Gospel. We must follow the call to live our lives for the kingdom.

This Week's Call to Action

Following the path of Christ means living a life of total surrender to the One who surrendered his life for us. This week, commit to taking meaningful action to live an unashamed Catholic life. Consider ways that you can put your family, your friends, and your Church before yourself. Spend time with Jesus celebrating your salvation and praying for the grace to persevere. Participate in the sacraments and seek out brothers for fellowship and support. Keep in mind the legacy we share as baptized Christians and work to take up your cross and follow more fully in the footsteps of Christ every day.

Our witness as Catholic men depends on our willingness to accept the call to follow Christ with all our minds, hearts, and souls. To be ashamed of Christ is to fail in our call to witness to the Gospel. We are either for Jesus or against him — so let us be firmly resolved to be for him in all things, no matter the cost.

SUNDAY

It can be hard to face ourselves when we are ashamed of Christ; but it is important to acknowledge our weaknesses so we can make a deeper commitment to sold-out Catholic living. This week, commit to denying yourself, taking up your cross, and following Christ, just as he commands. Seek to understand how the apparent contradictions of our faith are really profound truths when seen through heaven's eyes. Remember that the cost paid by Christ for our salvation is immeasurable and complete. We can rely on his grace to carry us through so that when Our Lord returns in glory, he will recognize us and welcome us into his kingdom.

This week at Mass, stand loud and proud as you sing, pray, and come to the table of the Lord. Meditate on the Eucharist as a sacrifice that we celebrate with joy and anticipation as we await Christ's return in glory. Pray honestly about those times when you were ashamed or halfhearted in your commitment to your Savior. Ask God to show you how you can grow in your walk with Jesus, how you can extend your unashamed love for the Gospel to others through works of charity, and how you can grow closer to God as you move from faith to faith, day by wonderful day.

Questions for reflection
What areas of your life do you hold back from Jesus?

How can you turn any doubt and shame you feel into confident surrender to the cause of Christ?

Praying with Scripture
"For I am not ashamed of the gospel: it is the power of God for salvation to every one who has faith, to the Jew first and also to the Greek" (Rom 1:16).

MONDAY
DENY YOURSELF, TAKE UP YOUR CROSS, AND FOLLOW CHRIST

While we were staying for some days, a prophet named Agabus came down from Judea. And coming to us he took Paul's belt and bound his own feet and hands, and said, "Thus says the Holy Spirit, 'So shall the Jews at Jerusalem bind the man who owns this belt and deliver him into the hands of the Gentiles.'" When we heard this, we and the people there begged him not to go up to Jerusalem. Then Paul answered, "What are you doing, weeping and breaking my heart? For I am ready not only to be imprisoned but even to die at Jerusalem for the name of the Lord Jesus." And when he would not be persuaded, we ceased and said, "The will of the Lord be done."

Acts 21:10–14

For Catholics, there can be no compromise when it comes to following Jesus. There are no halfway commitments, no hedging our bets. Like Paul, we must be willing to lay down our lives joyfully for the Lord. For most of us, this will not involve being executed for our beliefs. But it could very well mean enduring ridicule, the loss of friends, and personal suffering along the way of our salvation. Though many people speak of taking up their cross like some kind of personalized trial made especially for us, the central call of the cross is to surrender ourselves to the cause of Christ, to walk the rough road of life and to count it all joy (cf. Jas 1:2).

We are to be living sacrifices to God (cf. Rom 12:1), daily offering up our lives to the One who saved us from sin. Every word and deed for the Catholic man is meant to be a form of worship. We are called to lay our prayers, our actions, and our very lives on the altar of heaven, as we build the legacy of our faith for those who are members of the Church now and those who will come after us. We are servants who carry the Gospel to all people as we live out our salvation with joy.

Questions for reflection

How willing would you be to lay down your physical life for the Gospel?

In what ways are you laying down your life daily as a living sacrifice to please God?

How does taking up your cross daily help to lead others closer to Christ?

Praying with Scripture

"Therefore be imitators of God, as beloved children. And walk in love, as Christ loved us and gave himself up for us, a fragrant offering and sacrifice to God" (Eph 5:1–2).

TUESDAY
IT'S ALL OPPOSITES

But whatever gain I had, I counted as loss for the sake of Christ. Indeed I count everything as loss because of the surpassing worth of knowing Christ Jesus my Lord. For his sake I have suffered the loss of all things, and count them as refuse, in order that I may gain Christ and be found in him, not having a righteousness of my own, based on law, but that which is through faith in Christ, the righteousness from God that depends on faith; that I may know him and the power of his resurrection, and may share his sufferings, becoming like him in his death, that if possible I may attain the resurrection from the dead.

Philippians 3:7–11

It can seem so absurd: dying to live, being weak to find strength, and enduring our sufferings while counting it all joy. Our faith often appears all backward and upside down. The world tells us to be strong, to look out for number one, and to win by accumulating the most possessions and gaining the best position. Yet, as Catholics, we have been shown this incredibly better way, the way of the cross. As we surrender the self to God, we gain the entire universe. We are freed from the power of sin and given the power to overcome anything for the sake of the Gospel.

When we look at our faith through the lens of heaven, these opposites come into their right perspective. We see the absurdity of putting our insignificant earthly lives first, and we experience the joy that comes from receiving the Spirit of our

Savior. With joy we are willing to add our lives to the building up of the Church and leave a legacy that will inspire generations to come. We are able to discard our painful past and gaze upon new horizons of possibilities as we live for the Lord. In the end, we will experience the full reward of our salvation with all those who have chosen to lose all and gain Christ.

Questions for reflection
How have you experienced the profound truth of the seeming contradictions in the Gospel in your own life?

How do you explain the absurdity of the Gospel to those who oppose or ridicule it?

How can you share the power of the resurrection with someone else in your life today?

Praying with Scripture
"For to me to live is Christ, and to die is gain" (Phil 1:21).

WEDNESDAY
THERE IS NO COMPARISON IN THE COSTS

Then Peter said in reply, "Behold, we have left everything and followed you. What then shall we have?" Jesus said to them, "Truly, I say to you, in the new world, when the Son of man shall sit on his glorious throne, you who have followed me will also sit on twelve thrones, judging the twelve tribes of Israel. And every one who has left houses or brothers or sisters or father or mother or children or lands, for my name's sake, will receive a hundredfold, and inherit eternal life. But many that are first will be last, and the last first."

Matthew 19:27–30

The Twelve Apostles gave up their homes, their livelihood, and their safe, normal lives to follow Jesus. Jesus promised them unimaginable riches in the kingdom to come, and he makes that same promise to all who give up their lives to follow him. While we live on this earth, it may sometimes appear that we are not benefiting from our faith, but this is really what faith is all about. Christ gives us a peace that is greater than any possession or position, which we experience even now on earth. Moreover, we look forward to the eternal joy that awaits us in heaven.

There is no comparison between earthly pleasures and heavenly joys, our position in this life and our position in the life to come. We could store up for ourselves an abundance of wealth, but in the end, when our life is demanded of us, it will all mean nothing (cf. Lk 12:16–21). Our highest calling is to take our lives and lay them down before the throne of heaven — a testimony that will draw others into the kingdom. We are called to seek first that kingdom and all we desire will be ours (cf. Mt 6:33). When we put Our Lord before all things, we gain the greatest gift of all: an inheritance that we can pass on to others in the name of Jesus.

Questions for reflection
Do you ever find yourself comparing the costs when it comes to following Christ? Do you believe that the eternal happiness of heaven is worth any price?

What costs have you paid as a Catholic, and have those costs been worth it?

How can you walk with a brother who is struggling with the demands of faith right now?

Praying with Scripture
"For what will it profit a man, if he gains the whole world and forfeits his life? Or what shall a man give in return for his life?" (Mt 16:26).

THURSDAY
IF WE ARE ASHAMED OF CHRIST, HE WILL BE ASHAMED OF US

For I am not ashamed of the gospel: it is the power of God for salvation to every one who has faith, to the Jew first and also to the Greek. For in it the righteousness of God is revealed through faith for faith; as it is written, "He who through faith is righteous shall live."

Romans 1:16–17

Do not be ashamed then of testifying to our Lord, nor of me his prisoner, but take your share of suffering for the gospel in the power of God.

2 Timothy 1:8

Often we are tempted to be ashamed of our faith. When we hear people around us speaking against Christ, many of us keep silent, afraid to defend our Savior. Or perhaps we fail to put our faith into practice, neglecting the Gospel and its call to love as we have been loved by God. Jesus has a harsh word for those who call him Lord yet do not live for him: "I never knew you; depart from me, you evildoers" (cf. Mt 7:23). To be unashamed of Christ is to accept the trials that come our way and allow the grace of God to refine us day by day, from one experience to the next.

Being Catholic is an exercise in grace-filled living. Paul reminded Timothy of this by comparing a believer to a career soldier, a committed athlete, and a diligent farmer (cf. 2 Tm 2:1–7). All three are sold out to the goal set before them. All three work for something that endures and stands as a legacy of faith, whether achieving victory in battle, crossing the finish line, or reaping a bountiful harvest. Our spiritual lives are to manifest this same legacy of triumph and testimony. Being unashamed allows us to live fully what the Gospel is all about.

Questions for reflection

Have you experienced being ashamed of Christ? What was that like? How did you respond?

How can you deepen your commitment to the battles, goals, and harvests before you?

How can you accompany and help a brother who may be tempted to be ashamed of the Gospel?

Praying with Scripture

"Do your best to present yourself to God as one approved, a workman who has no need to be ashamed, rightly handling the word of truth" (2 Tm 2:15).

FRIDAY
CHRIST IS COMING INTO HIS GLORY

But we see Jesus, who for a little while was made lower than the angels, crowned with glory and honor because of the suffering of death, so that by the grace of God he might taste death for every one.

Hebrews 2:9

When Jesus returns to earth in his glory, he will greet us according to the deeds we have done, whether good or bad (cf. Mt 25:31–46). The Creed tells us, "He will come again in glory to judge the living and the dead." He who was placed lower than the heavenly beings and experienced death for the sake of humanity will one day stand before us all as our judge. What a blessed thought to know that those of us who are not ashamed of Christ will experience his presence in an eternal kingdom where sin and death will be no more.

On that wonderful day, we who have been saved by grace

will stand before our King and present the legacy of our lives as living sacrifices, holy and pleasing to God (cf. Rom 12:1). We await his return with joyful anticipation and lasting hope.

Questions for reflection
How does knowing that Christ will come again affect the way you live your Catholic faith?

In what ways are you working to live more fully an unashamed life that is pleasing to God?

How specifically can you work out your salvation in sacrificial service to others today?

Praying with Scripture
"And we all, with unveiled face, beholding the glory of the Lord, are being changed into his likeness from one degree of glory to another; for this comes from the Lord who is the Spirit" (2 Cor 3:18).

SATURDAY

Go Deeper
Have I put myself aside in order to take up my cross and follow Jesus this week? Were there times when I failed to do so?

_____

_____

_____

_____

Do I recognize that the apparent contradictions within my faith are actually profound truths? If I still struggle to see this, am I willing to accept it in faith?

_____

_____

_____

_____

What has it cost me so far to live for Christ? Do I believe that it is all worth it?

_____

_____

_____

_____

Have I been ashamed of Christ? How can I commit to serving him with courage and devotion from now on?

_____

_____

_____

_____

_____

Have I reached out to support others who may be tempted to be ashamed of the Gospel? Have I encouraged them to cling to the truth?

_____

_____

_____

_____

WEEK 10

WHERE DO WE GO FROM HERE?

Now the eleven disciples went to Galilee, to the mountain to which Jesus had directed them. And when they saw him they worshiped him; but some doubted. And Jesus came and said to them, "All authority in heaven and on earth has been given to me. Go therefore and make disciples of all nations, baptizing them in the name of the Father and of the Son and of the Holy Spirit, teaching them to observe all that I have commanded you; and behold, I am with you always, to the close of the age."

Matthew 28:16–20

Jesus sent his disciples out to the whole world to draw others into the Kingdom of God. That commission has continued in the Church down through the ages. We as Catholic men today share in that call. Being a witness for Jesus is a great responsibility, an incredible privilege, and an inexpressible joy. Christ calls us to be his hands and feet, eyes and ears, and his presence in our world.

This is the Great Commission. As members of the Church, we have the Holy Spirit to guide us in the work we do for the kingdom. Every prayer, every word, and every deed is a page in the story of our lives, written in the Lamb's book, laid open for others to see. We must understand the importance of leaving behind an example of solid, sold-out faith, a faith that inspires others to continue the journey, that builds up the Body of Christ, and gives honor and glory to God.

This week, we will reflect on the following:

1. Like the Apostles, we are called to follow Jesus.
As members of the Church, we have been called to follow in the footsteps of the Apostles, the martyrs, and all the saints. To be a witness for Christ is our heavenly goal. The story of our Catholic life should be a story any believer would want to hear. As we follow, so do we add to the story of the Church as she readies herself for the Wedding Feast when the Bridegroom comes again.

2. The response to God's call is either worship or doubt.
We can either fall in surrender before our King or reject him and turn away. Whatever our response, Jesus is still Lord. He continues to call all people to come to him, and he continues to call men to be his witnesses to the world. We must ask ourselves if our lives give testimony to the glory of the One who gave himself up for us, or if they speak only of our own selfishness and sad pride.

3. Jesus approaches us with authority.
Our Lord gave up his heavenly throne to live among us as a man, and he continues to approach his people with the same love that brought him down from heaven. Because of the cross, he — and he alone — has the authority to call us to follow. How we respond to that authority will determine the legacy we leave behind.

4. We are called to make disciples, baptize, and teach.
We have not been called to make conversions, but to make disciples. This means we are not only meant to lead people to Jesus; we must also be prepared to walk with them on the journey to heaven. We cannot simply check off a list of Catholic tasks. We must give our lives over to the cause of Christ and draw future generations into the Kingdom of God.

5. Christ is with us always.

Perhaps we should take the last sentence in Matthew's Gospel as a command: behold, Jesus is with us forever! Accepting that we have the presence of Christ to guide us is foundational to our witness in this world. Our every action in this life should bear the touch of his grace and shine before the Church and the world as we point the way to heaven for all who come seeking the Savior.

This Week's Call to Action

As Catholic men, we share an incredible legacy in the Church. We have the Holy Spirit as our counselor, the word of God as our comfort, and the teachings of the Church as our commission. This week, make a deeper commitment to step into this legacy, standing side by side with your brothers in the faith. Empowered by the Spirit, informed by the Gospel, and nourished by the sacraments, pledge to shine your light before all the world. Take Christ's commission seriously and live it out joyfully, knowing that your greatest reward is yet to come.

Remember: one day, we will see the fruit of our efforts, the result of our faith and charitable work for the Gospel. What a glorious day that will be!

SUNDAY

This week we will reflect on our call to follow in the footsteps of Jesus, choosing life over death, carrying the Gospel to the ends of the earth as we make disciples for Christ. Making disciples is a lifetime commitment, and this journey connects us to brothers who walk this way of discipleship with us. Moreover, we have Jesus' assurance that he is with us as well — forever.

As you celebrate the Eucharist this Sunday, take note especially of the last call from the altar: to go forth to serve the Lord and one another. Let the calling you have received make you mindful of this blessed commission to share the Gospel with the world as you join in the prayers, hear the word of God, and receive the Body and Blood of Christ. Pray about what it means to share this great legacy of our faith with your brothers, and to prepare future generations to receive this same gift. Consider how you will go forward in your walk with Christ accompanied by your brothers within the body of believers. Make a deeper commitment to God, and ask him to show you how he wants you to serve him. Ask him for the grace to continue to serve him in love all the days of your life.

Questions for reflection

Do you recognize that you have an important part to play in the Great Commission?

How can you and your brothers join together to answer Christ's call in your local church?

Praying with Scripture

"He who testifies to these things says, 'Surely I am coming soon.' Amen. Come, Lord Jesus!" (Rv 22:20).

MONDAY
LIKE THE APOSTLES, WE ARE CALLED TO FOLLOW JESUS

If any one serves me, he must follow me; and where I am, there shall my servant be also; if any one serves me, the Father will honor him.

John 12:26

My sheep hear my voice, and I know them, and they follow me; and I give them eternal life, and they shall never perish, and no one shall snatch them out of my hand. My Father, who has giv-

*en them to me, is greater than all, and no one is able to snatch
them out of the Father's hand. I and the Father are one.*

John 10:27–30

We cannot be disciples of Jesus unless we follow in his footsteps
to Calvary, draw from his grace, and celebrate our resurrected
life in him. He calls us to join the commission he gave to his
Apostles: to go out into the world and share the Good News.

Do you hear the voice of your Shepherd calling? Are you
willing to venture out into the wilderness of life and trust that
the Lord will never allow anyone to snatch you out of his hand?
Will you promise to serve with your whole heart, totally committed to the journey of salvation, from now straight on into
eternity? We have been given a great gift. We are loved by a
Savior who left the mansions of heaven to walk the dusty roads
of this earth, suffered at the hands of evil men, and died on the
cruel cross to save us from our sins. Let us not waste our legacy,
but go forward with great anticipation and exuberant joy as we
dedicate our lives to the cause of Christ.

Questions for reflection
What does it mean to follow Jesus? How has following Jesus
shaped (and changed) your life?

Where do you hear the voice of the Good Shepherd calling you
to go in the days to come?

How will you continue to share the gift of salvation with all
those around you?

Praying with Scripture
"For to this you have been called, because Christ also suffered
for you, leaving you an example, that you should follow in his
steps" (1 Pt 2:21).

TUESDAY
THE RESPONSE TO GOD'S CALL IS EITHER WORSHIP OR DOUBT

"See, I have set before you this day life and good, death and evil. If you obey the commandments of the LORD your God which I command you this day, by loving the LORD your God, by walking in his ways, and by keeping his commandments and his statutes and his ordinances, then you shall live and multiply, and the LORD your God will bless you in the land which you are entering to take possession of it. But if your heart turns away, and you will not hear, but are drawn away to worship other gods and serve them, I declare to you this day, that you shall perish; you shall not live long in the land which you are going over the Jordan to enter and possess. I call heaven and earth to witness against you this day, that I have set before you life and death, blessing and curse; therefore choose life, that you and your descendants may live, loving the LORD your God, obeying his voice, and clinging to him; for that means life to you and length of days, that you may dwell in the land which the LORD swore to your fathers, to Abraham, to Isaac, and to Jacob, to give them."

Deuteronomy 30:15–20

The choice may appear to be complicated, but it is truly simple. We have before us life or death, heaven or hell, joy or misery, blessing or curse. Yes, following in the footsteps of Jesus will not always be easy or convenient. In this world, we will experience trouble, trials, and tribulation. But the promises and the commands of the Lord are clear: Choose life and find eternity and joy, or choose death and find everlasting torment and despair. There is no third choice.

As a Catholic man, living out your faith in Christ, you have seen how Jesus carries you through the tough times. You have witnessed how he overcomes fear with faith, grief with grace, and sorrow with salvation. You have seen the power that is yours when you surrender your life and accept the gifts he gives you. This is your inheritance, an inheritance you are called to proclaim to all the world by your words, your deeds, and your very life.

Questions for reflection

In your life, have you tried to follow a way other than *the* Way, Jesus himself? What was the result?

What blessings has God given you as you have committed to follow him?

How can you support a brother who may be tempted to turn from worship to doubt?

Praying with Scripture

"For the wages of sin is death, but the free gift of God is eternal life in Christ Jesus our Lord" (Rom 6:23).

WEDNESDAY
JESUS APPROACHES US WITH AUTHORITY

He who comes from above is above all; he who is of the earth belongs to the earth, and of the earth he speaks; he who comes from heaven is above all. He bears witness to what he has seen and heard, yet no one receives his testimony; he who receives his testimony sets his seal to this, that God is true. For he whom God has sent utters the words of God, for it is not by measure that he gives the Spirit; the Father loves the Son, and has given all things into his hand. He who believes in the Son has eternal life; he who does not obey the Son shall not see life, but the wrath of God rests upon him.

John 3:31–36

Our Lord's sacrifice for our sins has exalted him to the highest place (cf Phil 2:9), and we have been given membership in his Mystical Body. We are new creatures, purposed for great works of service in the Kingdom of God. All of this is because Jesus, the One from above, has the power and authority over all things.

Moreover, Jesus is fully human and fully divine. His divinity was never diminished by his human life here among us. All the fullness of God, all the power of the universe, all the wisdom of eternity dwells in him. He shares his authority with us through our baptism and the daily grace we receive from him. Thus he gives us victory over sin, insight for understanding the Gospel, and power to change lives in the name of Jesus. He is our God and deserves our whole life. This is the great legacy we have been given: to share the love of Jesus with others by how we carry on his calling in our lives.

Questions for reflection

Where have you seen the greatest sign of Christ's love in your life?

How does living under the authority of Jesus give you freedom for holy living?

Where do you believe God is leading you in your walk with his Son?

Praying with Scripture

"For in him the whole fullness of deity dwells bodily, and you have come to fullness of life in him, who is the head of all rule and authority" (Col 2:9–10).

THURSDAY
WE ARE CALLED TO MAKE DISCIPLES, BAPTIZE, AND TEACH

But how are men to call upon him in whom they have not believed? And how are they to believe in him of whom they have never heard? And how are they to hear without a preacher? And how can men preach unless they are sent? As it is written, "How beautiful are the feet of those who preach good news!"

Romans 10:14–15

And he said to them, "Go into all the world and preach the gospel to the whole creation. He who believes and is baptized will be saved; but he who does not believe will be condemned."

Mark 16:15–16

Some Christians seem to focus solely on converting the lost. The truth is, we are called to make disciples, baptizing them and teaching them to observe all that God commands (cf. Mt 28:19–20). Our call as Catholic men is not simply to help save souls, but to walk with brothers and sisters along the way of salvation. It is a glorious thing to see someone turn from their sin and believe in the Gospel. It is even more glorious to continue the journey with another, moment to moment along the narrow path to heaven's shining shores.

The way to heaven can seem like a lonely walk, but not if we are willing to enter into the day-to-day experiences of others and share the teachings of our faith and the grace that empowers us to become citizens of the kingdom. We are to lead others to the table and the confessional, to help them grow in the knowledge of Christ, and to leave their mark upon the Church and the world along with us. As we are willing to go where the lost reside, so can the Gospel go forth into the world to rescue sinners and lead them home.

Questions for reflection

What is the difference between making converts and making disciples?

What has been one of your most memorable moments in walking with others for Christ?

How has the Church supported you in word and sacrament over the years?

Praying with Scripture

"But you shall receive power when the Holy Spirit has come upon you; and you shall be my witnesses in Jerusalem and in all Judea and Samaria and to the end of the earth" (Acts 1:8).

FRIDAY
CHRIST IS WITH US ALWAYS

If you love me, you will keep my commandments. And I will ask the Father, and he will give you another Counselor, to be with you for ever, even the Spirit of truth, whom the world cannot receive, because it neither sees him nor knows him; you know him, for he dwells with you, and will be in you. I will not leave you desolate; I will come to you. Yet a little while, and the world will see me no more, but you will see me; because I live, you will live also. In that day you will know that I am in my Father, and you in me, and I in you.

John 14:15–20

Jesus promised to be with us forever (cf. Mt 28:20). He is "Emmanuel," God with us — meaning his coming into our lives is not a temporary thing. He did not come to earth thousands of years ago to speak some encouraging words to a few people and then go back home to heaven. He came for all time and for all people. This is the foundation of all our actions as believers. We are living out the joyful reality that God is with us in every moment, every word, every deed, and every hope.

The Holy Spirit has been given to us as guarantee of what is to come (cf. 2 Cor 1:22). He is our advocate, our teacher, our empowering strength, and our unending joy. Because he lives in us, we have all we need to complete the good work God has given us to do. We are no longer wandering orphans, cut off from heaven, and dead in our sins. We are saints set apart for the divine purposes to which God has called us. We are one in Spirit with the Son of God!

Questions for reflection
Where have you experienced God's presence most fully in your life?

When you struggle to recognize God's presence, where do you turn?

How can you help a brother who may be struggling to believe in Christ's enduring presence in his life right now?

Praying with Scripture
"Have I not commanded you? Be strong and of good courage; be not frightened, neither be dismayed; for the LORD your God is with you wherever you go." (Jos 1:9)

SATURDAY

Go Deeper

Have I responded with generosity to Christ's commission, or am I holding back in any way? If I am holding back — why?

_____

_____

_____

_____

Have I given in to doubt? Where do I need the Lord to strengthen my faith?

_____

_____

_____

_____

Do I act on the authority and power of Jesus as I share the Gospel with others?

_____

_____

_____

_____

Am I helping to make disciples, or do I leave that up to others? Where is the Lord calling me to share the Gospel?

_____

_____

_____

Do I believe that Christ is truly present in my life, or do I doubt his word? Where do I experience his presence most fully?

_____

_____

_____

Do I seek merely to make converts, or am I working to make disciples, willing to accompany them on the journey of faith?

_____

_____

_____

Conclusion

A new commandment I give to you, that you love one another; even as I have loved you, that you also love one another. By this all men will know that you are my disciples, if you have love for one another.

John 13:34–35

The journey is not over. It will continue until our Lord and Savior comes again in all his glory. In the meantime, we are doing what we were created and called to do: to be disciples and to make disciples. Our membership in the Church Christ founded is our great legacy, and we are called to invite everyone we meet into this same inheritance. Who we are in Christ should spill out from our hearts to our lips, our hands, and our feet as we walk the path to heaven and love others along the way.

I encourage you to continue what you have begun here. Be deliberate in reaching out to your brothers with the message of hope that Jesus offers. Continue to take time to study God's word and grow together in your faith. Receive the sacraments often and join in the celebration of the Eucharist each Sunday with commitment, conviction, and joy. Never be ashamed of Christ, but strive to live out your Catholic faith in all you say and do. Love your family and the family of faith well. Confront sin in yourself and speak truth into the lives of others, particularly your brothers in Christ. Seek your Savior, bless the broken, and grow in grace. Cherish your faith and work out your salvation with fear and trembling as you delight in what it means to be a Catholic man.

God bless you in this journey of discipleship, from where you live to the very ends of the earth!

ACKNOWLEDGMENTS

Mary Beth Baker, you took on this project with incredible skill, insight, and grace, and helped to turn it into what it is today. Thank you for being bold enough to nudge me in new directions, for showing incredible patience, and most of all for treating my book as if it were the only one you were editing. You brought balance and focus to my vision. Our Sunday Visitor has been blessed by your dedication and love for the Lord.

Laura Wolfskill, you deserve a medal for poring over my manuscript looking for repeated Bible verses and strange turns of phrase. Thank you and your team for making me look good and for all the many little details you handled to make this project a success. You are my hero!

Jaymie Wolfe, thank you for seeing the potential in a manuscript that grew from a simple devotional into a God-honoring and beautiful Bible study. You took the seed and planted it, and now the harvest has come!

Our Sunday Visitor, bless you for all those Sunday School lessons I loved as a boy and used as a children's minister. It is an honor to have been brought into the family to share with others what those lessons have produced in me.

Ken Santopietro, who invited me to serve on the planning committee of the Connecticut Catholic Men's Conference — you are a true example of a selfless and caring Catholic man.

My little online musings for the conference became this book and your support helped to carry me through.

My wife, Christina, and my three children, Adam Mark, Lina Rose, and Hope Elizabeth, you have continued to love a husband and father who is forever a work in progress. You are my joy, my strength, and my constant comfort. Thank you for your love and support through all the years.

Ines Davino, my wonderful mother-in-law, you gave me that first copy of the magazine that helped to revive my writing career. You never stopped believing in me and supporting my gift for words. Though I dedicated this work to your husband, I know his character has been shaped by the love and support that you have always shown him.

ABOUT THE AUTHOR

MARK C. MCCANN is an author and ministry consultant with over thirty years of ministry experience to children, youth, and families on the parish and diocesan level. He has also worked as a host and producer on Christian radio and written for a number of Catholic magazines and websites, including *St. Anthony Messenger*, *Emmanuel Magazine*, and *Catholic Stand*. He lives in Connecticut with his Proverbs 31 wife and has three incredible children. Each day he follows his call to be a man of words. You can learn about Mark's writing and ministry by going to www.wordsnvisions.com.